D0932835

A corporate satire as outrageous as a $6,000 shower curtain

THE CEO

AN INTERACTIVE BOOK

OWEN BURKE AND DUFF McDONALD

SIMON SPOTLIGHT ENTERTAINMENT

New York London Toronto Sydney

If you purchased this book without a cover, you should be aware that this book is stolen property. It was reported as "unsold and destroyed" to the publisher, and neither the author nor the publisher has received any payment for this "stripped book."

This book is a work of fiction. Any references to historical events, real people, or real locales are used fictitiously. Other names, characters, places, and incidents are the product of the author's imagination, and any resemblance to actual events or locales or persons, living or dead, is entirely coincidental.

SSE SIMON SPOTLIGHT ENTERTAINMENT
An imprint of Simon & Schuster
1230 Avenue of the Americas, New York, New York 10020
Text copyright © 2005 by Owen Burke and Duff McDonald
All rights reserved, including the right of reproduction in whole or in part in any form.
SIMON SPOTLIGHT ENTERTAINMENT and related logo are trademarks of Simon & Schuster, Inc.
Manufactured in the United States of America
First Edition 10 9 8 7 6 5 4 3 2 1
Library of Congress Control Number 2004023517
ISBN 1-4169-0044-6

ACKNOWLEDGMENTS

This book could not have been written without the support of our editor, Tricia Boczkowski, who made the executive decision to take on this challenge. Thanks also to the women who love us enough to put up with us.

For Martha, Dennis, Kenneth, Jack & Suzie, and John & his sons—we couldn't have done it without you.

You never thought it would happen.

Friends have gone back to Iowa to work on their dads' farms, former partners are working in tire shops—you, on the other hand, have ridden bulls and fought bears in the dog-eat-dog world of business. You did it by making a product that practically sells itself, a product that actually lives up to its hype. It's the ultimate gear for the twenty-first-century survivor: the Silk Armor clothing line. The fabric feels like your coolest summer shirt or your coziest winter sweater, but there's more. . . . It's waterproof, windproof, fireproof, *and* bulletproof.

You are the CEO of Fleece Industries, the subject of numerous profiles in the business press, the hometown hero, and the envy of clothing executives the world over. You are, in short, the hottest clothing manufacturer since the invention of the toga. And today you're taking your company public.

Your life's work—building a business from an idea scrawled on a bar napkin into a world-renowned clothing empire—has reached a major milestone: You're going to have an initial public offering, or IPO, on the New York Stock Exchange. Everyone will soon be able to buy shares in Fleece Industries. You, personally, will be the owner of ten million shares out of a total of fifteen million, or 66 percent. The ticker symbol: CON.

Your wife has accompanied you to the exchange for the opening bell on the first day of the trading of your stock. She is pretty; you married her because she looks like the kind of woman who would marry an astronaut. A woman of simple values and tenacious loyalty, she has been with you from the start. She has seen the good times and the bad. The two of you have flown to Paris for a weekend, and you have also shared a can of tuna when your power was shut off. Now you're sitting in a town car on Broad Street outside the exchange, looking down at her fingers intertwined with your own.

"I know this sounds silly, honey, but this all reminds me of our wedding day," she says.

"I feel it too," you respond, clutching her hand. "This is very exciting. . . . It's a very happy time for both of us."

"The difference is that we couldn't have afforded a car like this back then," she says. "Remember when Bobby lent us his Oldsmobile Cutlass, and it broke down between the reception and the hotel?"

"I carried you the whole way."

"Half the way . . . but I appreciated the gesture," she responds.

"Maybe we should go back to that hotel and renew our vows," you say, not really thinking about it, but trying to make small talk while you consider the millions of dollars you will soon be worth.

"Honey, that hotel was a dump," she says.

"Fine," you respond. "Let's buy the place and have it knocked down."

All of a sudden the door of your car is opened. "I think it's time," you say to your wife.

It is indeed time. You are at Broad and Wall, the nexus of American capitalism, at the door of the New York Stock Exchange. You step out of the car and walk through the labyrinth of police barriers on the sidewalk to go through security.

Standing on the other side of the metal detector is the chairman of the exchange, Ricky Dey, a short bald man with a glistening dome so shiny you can see your own reflection in it. You wonder, momentarily, what the official definition of a midget is, and then it hits you—he looks exactly like the mad scientist Dr. Sivana, Captain Marvel's archnemesis from those old 1940s comic books. The image makes you smile as you reach out to shake his hand. He is wearing a black pin-striped suit that you can only imagine was custom fit to his diminutive body somewhere in Europe. It occurs to you that your Brooks Brothers suit might be inadequate.

Your intuition is dead-on. "Congratulations," he says, handing you his tailor's card. He stares at your tie for a little too long, and then looks you in the eye and says, "Welcome to the club."

The club's members are some of the most successful, influential, and inspirational people who ever lived. From J. P. Morgan to Michael Eisner to Crazy Eddie Antar, the NYSE has been the true birthplace of American success stories. The laws are made in Washington, but the money is made here, and any trader will tell you that "money is always above the law."

As you ride the elevator with Ricky Dey beside you and your wife clutching your arm, you can barely contain your excitement.

"Gum?" asks Ricky, holding a stick of Doublemint gum up to you.

"No thanks." You are too nervous to chew anything.

"Hard candy?" Ricky says, pulling a piece out of his pocket.

"I'm good."

"Toffee?

"I'm a little too anxious to be putting anything in my mouth," you reply with a nervous laugh.

"Especially your foot." Ricky is genuinely doing his best to calm you. "Slim Jim?"

15 ↑1.75 ADLAC 22 ↓ 2.60 ENE 50.50 ↑1.50 TYC 60.25 ↓ 1.75 MSO 65 ↑ 2.5

Go to page 6.

Just then the waiter arrives with your martini. You stand up, grab it off the tray, chug the whole thing, and stare at Barry and then at Moneyhouse. "To hell with you both." You slam down your glass and walk out the door onto Wall Street. The sun hits your eyes the same way it does any man who has been drinking in a dark bar before he's even had lunch. Weiss? Could he really have been crooked? But why? The company was doing so well. Or was it . . . ?

You jump into a cab and head back to the office. You call Fawn and instruct her to deactivate Barry's security pass, tell the front desk not to let him in the building, shut down his e-mail, and put his computer in the company vault. You also tell her to have the IT people freeze Weiss's computer and have security take him into your office and keep him there.

Your phone rings. It's your wife. You don't have time to talk to her and let it go to voice mail. It rings again. It's Barry. Screw him. He's dead to you now. You're the only one you can trust at this point. Your phone rings again. Moneyhouse, that bastard. Screw him, too.

15 ↑1.75 ADLAC 22 ↓2.60 ENE 50.50 ↑1.50 TYC 60.25 ↓1.75 MSO 65 ↑2.5

Go to page 79.

McDougal begins slowly and deliberately. "Spring will be hot this year. We've just cut a deal with the people at the Australian Open. They want to give the tourney a sexier image like the French Open has. We're outfitting everyone from the players to the ball boys and giving the judges bulletproof sweater-vests—with the calls they make, they're going to need them."

Araz springs from the wall and starts moving about the room again. "We're working with Nicole Kidman's people to try to get her and Naomi Watts to wear Fleece to the matches." He has rolled up the magazine and is swatting it like a racket, playing an imaginary tennis match around your office.

"Better go through Naomi's people; she's easier to get to and can influence Nicole," McDougal says into his coffee cup.

"Exactly!" Araz yells, pointing at McDougal. "And we've got Briana Ponastova. Since she quit tennis to be a model, we have her under contract to walk around stadiums in Fleece outfits like a roving mannequin."

"Guys, this is great! I'm so happy. Thank you. We're going to make Fleece synonymous with all that is sexy about tennis and all that is safe with tournament security! Geniuses! You guys are geniuses! Now get out of here before I decide to double your salaries! I've got some IPO stuff to finish up."

Araz pushes Jeff out of the office. Those guys are nuts, but they're genuine alchemists. They just solved another problem for you. Will their talents never cease?

Go to page 243.

You're standing on the balcony of the exchange, a venue that has been occupied by every big shot in the history of American business. Looking at the sea of floor traders below, you briefly experience what you can describe only as a combination of time-lessness and vertigo. You know from watching CNBC that as soon as the bell rings, all hell will break loose in front of your eyes.

You look down and notice that Dey is standing on a pile of phone books. You decide not to say anything, instead filing the information away for the tell-all business book, *How to Get Really Rich*, that you're planning to write after you retire. Dey gives the signal and you ring the bell. Cheers erupt. Your stock's symbol passes across the ticker tape right there in the heart of the exchange. It has opened trading at ten dollars a share. That makes you worth $100 million at this very moment. After shaking hands with a dozen people you don't know or care about, you are escorted out of the exchange. You put your wife into the town car, sending her home, and climb into a limo with a hand-ful of adoring Fleece employees.

Sitting in the car, a bottle of champagne is uncorked and the bubbly is passed around despite it being only 9:45 on a Monday morning. The world is your oyster. The car pulls away from the curb, and everything dissolves into a blur of laughter as com-muters whiz past the car windows.

Your car drives up Eighth Avenue, and even though it's the usual bumper-to-bumper traffic crawling uptown, your limou-sine seems to just blow on by all the jammed cars. The driver makes a right onto Forty-fourth Street, and you approach Times Square, where you see a large crowd of teenagers gath-ering outside MTV Studios.

"This is going to be great!" you say to everyone in the car. You take a big pull from the champagne bottle and instruct your driver to pull over and pop the trunk. You jump out of the lim-ousine like a movie star, to the excitement of the teenagers—

until they realize that they have no idea who you are.

You grab a big box out of the trunk and drop it on the side-walk. You open it up and start pulling out the green T-shirts you had made for this day that read: FLEECE WENT PUBLIC TODAY AND ALL I GOT WAS THIS LOUSY T-SHIRT! Within thirty seconds every-one in Times Square is advertising Fleece clothing. Everyone except the Naked Cowboy because, as he puts it, "It would go against my aesthetic." He agrees to pose for a picture with you, but insists that you drop your pants. You oblige because today you can do no wrong. You also have a slight champagne buzz.

You hop back in the car and everyone is clapping and cheer-ing you on. You take another swig of champagne and check your BlackBerry for the latest stock price. From the initial price of ten dollars, it already shot up to eighteen. Jesus! You're worth nearly $200 million. This is your day!

15 ↑ 1.75 ADLAC 22 ↓ 2.60 ENE 50.50 ↑ 1.50 TYC 60.25 ↓ 1.75 MSO 65 ↑ 2.50

Go to page 136.

You look at Jennifer sitting across from you, and you cannot remember a time when you were more disgusted with another human being. But this is business, and business is survival.

"Okay, Jennifer, slash the prices and book the sales for this quarter, and we'll deal with next quarter later. If this doesn't work, though, you and I are both destroyed."

"Threats are the song of the weak." Jennifer stands up, grabs the box of cookies she gave you, and walks out of the room.

Six months later you cannot believe your good fortune. Not only did the channel stuffing help you hit last year's sales targets, but also the effect of slashing your product from boutique prices to mass-market, middle-America hayseed price levels made Fleece's name as household as Kleenex. Your new low warehouse pricing strategy earned Fleece the distinction of being the fastest-growing publicly traded business in the country. Sales shoot through the roof, and your next two quarters are the most profitable in your company's history.

Depending on what business magazine you read, Jennifer Estrangelo is either a genius who masterminded how to make America wear Fleece, or an amazing salesperson who thrived under your strong leadership. Let her have her glory. Even though she made the mess, she cleaned it up too. And now she's someone else's problem, as she has since jumped ship to your biggest competitor. Donny Scott would have gotten her job, but Estrangelo fired him the moment she left your office that fateful day.

So much for playing by the rules.

The end

You head to your desk to sift through your messages. So many people have called to wish you the best, half of whom, you suspect, are hoping to be included in your newfound fortune.

Your cousin Pete, who used to own a chop shop in Milwaukee, wants you to come visit after all these years. Todd Toomie from UVA wants you to be the godfather to his unborn son. You guess he forgot that he tried to sleep with your wife six years ago. The pastor from your childhood town's parish wants your input on a bake sale to raise money for a new altar. You guess he forgot why you left the church in the first place.

Tyree Stubbs called you as well. Tyree plays basketball for the Los Angeles Terminators. He's the most dominating power forward under six feet in the history of the NBA and has led his team to three consecutive championships. Tyree also moonlights as a major rap star in the off-season and goes by the alias Three Point. His first album, "In Da Paint," was an enormous crossover hit, appealing to all races and both sexes. He is a notorious playboy and consummate bachelor, claiming to have had sex with fifteen thousand women and counting. Tyree wears Silk Armor exclusively, and you've created the "Stubby" line for Fleece, which is popular among inner-city youth. You met Tyree at the Seventh on Sixth Fashion Show and hit it off immediately. Ever since then, every time you get a call from him, it's either about an exclusive party, seats on the floor at a Knicks game, or backstage passes for bands and rappers of which you've never heard, but for whom your teenage daughter, Apple, goes crazy.

The last message is so out of the blue that you feel a hot rush of blood fill your face.

IMPORTANT MESSAGE

FOR _____

DATE _____ TIME 9:47 A.M./P.M.

WHILE YOU WERE OUT

M _____

OF _____

PHONE NO. 212-555-9826

TELEPHONED		PLEASE CALL	
CALLED TO SEE YOU		WILL CALL AGAIN	✓
WANTS TO SEE YOU		RUSH	
	RETURNED YOUR CALL		

MESSAGE

Aaron Rampstein

15 ↑ 1.75 ADLAC 22 ↓ 2.60 ENE 50.50 ↑

Go to page 149.

McDougal and Matali are waiting outside your office when you arrive back at 666 Madison Avenue. These two are as vital to the success of Fleece as anyone else. Araz pushed for low-rise capri pants while the rest of your competitors were only looking at the bottom hemline, and Jeff stopped wearing his Von Dutch trucker hat about two months before anyone in America even *began* wearing them. Their ability to see a trend before it's even begun has put Fleece out in front of the pack on more than one occasion.

McDougal is in his usual uniform: shabby chic business attire, a wide striped tie, and a colorful dress shirt. Matali, whose taste is as eclectic as McDougal's is grounded, is wearing running shorts and a vintage PITTSBURGH STEELERS #1 T-shirt. Only Matali, with his slick, jet black hair and green eyes, could pull off that outfit and somehow make it seem somewhat professional.

"Boys, have I got news for you," you say. "Come into my office." They follow you inside and take seats on opposite ends of your couch. Jeff throws a pen to Araz before he can ask for it, and they both wait expectantly for your plan for Fleece's new direction.

Perched on the corner of your desk, you break into the idea of Harry and how you will be the face of it all. After a few minutes of astonished silence from the two of them, you get the sense that they're already warming to the idea of making you the centerpiece of the company's marketing strategy going forward. Even if they don't think it's a good idea, they're smart enough not to fight you on it.

Araz jumps off the couch and throws Jeff's pen at him. "I have an idea! Let's get you a bear! All of the print campaigns, TV ads, hell, we'll put a bear face—"

"Or paw," interjects Jeff in a monotone voice from the couch.

"Or paw, on the clothes themselves! You know, as a logo!

Harry pals around with a bear! It's genius!" Araz is now running around the room as if he's taking a victory lap.

"I love it! As long as the bear doesn't take away from my image, I think it's great!" you say.

"The bear will only enhance your image. The bear will be a friendly reminder that you exist," Jeff mutters into his clipboard as if he is trying to conceal the bullshit by hiding his face.

"Araz! Go get the whiteboard and let's hammer out some ideas. I love the creative process! It's so much more rewarding than crunching numbers!"

Araz returns with the dry erase board, and the three of you go to work. Several hours later, well into the evening, there are Thai food containers, empty cans of Diet Coke, and discarded bottles of Heineken everywhere.

You are wearing mountain climbing gear, your seventh wardrobe change in the past three hours. Jeff insisted that you actually change clothes to help shake up the brainstorming session. You've worn exercise clothing, fishing gear, Fleece pajamas, a Fleece tuxedo, ski gear, and even a wet suit.

"We can do a photo shoot on the slopes of Kilimanjaro," says Araz. "And maybe we use it for billboards that are really high up, like on the sides of bridges or on the tops of buildings."

"Right," says Jeff. "We run the tuxedo ad in *Vogue* and the ski gear in *Outside* magazine, and we'll do an underwater film shoot for the wet suit and air the television commercial on ESPN."

"Maybe we can turn your life into a kind of long-running commercial," says Araz. "We follow you as you go hunting, fishing, skiing, and scuba diving."

"Interesting," you say, "but it's not like I actually do any of those things. That's all part of the secret. Fleece clothes are aspirational."

"So, what if we just follow you as you walk around the office, looking good in the everyday world?" asks Jeff.

The three of you all stop moving—and talking—at exactly the same time. That's it! That's the key to this whole idea. You're going to be the subject of a reality TV show.

15 ↑1.75 ADLAC 22 ↓2.60 ENE 50.50 ↑1.50 TYC 60.25 ↓1.75 MSO 65 ↑2.5

Do you think it's wise to base a television show on your daily life? Go to page 139.

Or do you stick to what you do best—running a clothing company? Go to page 94.

Your wife, meanwhile, seems to have gone off her rocker in a slightly different way from your own journey into narcissism.

After making friends with an organic farmer in the Hudson Valley, she falls in with a group of people skilled in the art of fortune-telling by means of examining the entrails of animals. It's not like they actually kill anything; rather, they drive around heavily wooded areas of New York state looking for roadkill and then inspect it on the spot.

After you plead with her to give up the practice—it would be a disaster to have the press find out your wife spends her days poking sticks into the still-warm bodies of dead deer and hedgehogs—she embarks on an unending exploration of the arts of divination. Aeromancy (the study of clouds), aleuromancy (fortune cookies), alomancy (table salt), austromancy (wind), critomancy (barley cakes), ichthyomancy (fish), onychomancy (fingernails), tiromancy (cheese), and margaritomancy (bouncing pearls). You put your foot down with the last one, as she begins buying expensive necklaces from Tiffany and destroying them in the foyer of your apartment in hopes of finding meaning.

She finally finds use for all her newfound insights, becoming a life coach under the name Fast Current, and actually lands a number of celebrity clients, including America's perkiest talk show host. You're just happy that she hasn't become the story of an E! special on rich people gone mad.

Apple watches both you and your wife with a sort of bemused detachment. She's happy about the increased level of access your rising star has given her, but she can't seem to come to terms with the fact that her own father is considered hip. She is equally incredulous of your wife's growing eccentricities. While at first she invites the Marriott sisters, friends from school, over to watch a barley cake reading or two, the embarrassment of having her own mother speak in tongues in front of her friends is too much. She's been spending a lot more time out of the house ever since.

15 ↑ 1.75 ADLAC 22 ↓ 2.60 ENE 50.50 ↑ 1.50 TYC 60.25 ↓ 1.75 MSO 65 ↑ 2.5

Go to page 74.

You tell Simpson to pick up Homer. Although it will add to the $600 million you've already borrowed, the debt seems worth it.

Simpson was right. As soon as word gets out that you've signed Homer, sales of Fleece products shoot through the roof. You are savvy enough to have a Homer jersey ready for sale the moment word breaks, and you sell 750,000 units in a single day.

The $10 million signing bonus you have to pay Homer boosts your personal borrowings to $610 million, but when you forecast the increase in ticket sales for the Argonauts as a result of signing him, you're comfortable that you'll be able to pay the players' salaries going forward through ticket receipts, the team's TV licensing, and merchandising. Hell, you'll probably be able to start paying down the loan sooner than you thought. You feel like a genius.

Homer, on the other hand, is a class-A moron. He drives his car to the wrong stadium on the first day. But, boy, can he throw the football. In his first game with the team Homer throws five touchdown passes and rushes for another touchdown himself. You blow out the Chicago Grizzlies 42 to 0.

The team is now 1 and 3.

When you wake up on the Monday after that first exhilarating game as an owner, you realize that you haven't been paying as much attention to Fleece as you should have in the past few weeks. When you get to your office that day, you put in a call to Alan Baldacker, your chief financial officer, to get an update on how things are going. The way you're feeling, you wouldn't be surprised if Fleece was also "undefeated" this year.

Go to page 19.

You turn off your monitor and decide it's time to leave the office for today. You're on the verge of a nervous breakdown anyway. Barry, especially, will know that something is up if he sees the state you're in. You pack your stuff, wash your face in your private bathroom, and head for the door.

Fawn looks up. "Where are you going? You have an eleven o'clock meeting with . . . um . . . Hey! What's wrong with your electronic calendar? Everything is gone! It was there a few minutes ago!"

For God's sake. You have always been a disaster on the computer, but you really don't need this right now.

"Fawn, I'm not feeling very well. I'm going home for the day. As for what's wrong with my calendar, I have no idea. Call the IT department. Tell them to earn their fucking salaries." And with that, you leave an open-mouthed Fawn staring at you as you walk down the hall.

The next day when you arrive at work, Barry is sitting in your office. At your desk.

"Hi, chief. How was your 'sick day'?"

"Fine, Barry, what do you want? Get out from behind my desk."

"Oh, nothing. Just scoping out my new office."

"What are you talking about?"

"After you left yesterday, I was talking to Fawn. She mentioned in passing that your electronic calendar had gone down. The IT guys told her that you'd inadvertently left your keyboard stuck on 'delete' of a certain meeting you and I had last week. So I got to thinking. Why would he delete that? And then I remembered how you were acting yesterday morning. So I called Felix. And guess what he told me?"

You're screwed.

"What did he tell you, Barry?"

"The same thing I told the board in a conference call yesterday afternoon. We can either announce your resignation this morning or your firing this afternoon. It's up to you. Oh, and your stock has been seized. Why'd you buy it back, by the way? It would have been much harder for us to take the cash back from you. Plus, you bought it at a higher price. What kind of fool are you?"

In the end, public opinion of you drops further than that of Om Daddy. Not only did you not care enough about the safety of the nation's soldiers that you kept the news of the T-shirts a secret while you tried to salvage your fortune, but also you were caught dead to rights committing insider trading.

Barry plays his part like a pro. He tells investigators that he had tried to convince you to make the announcement and that you'd promised to do so. He claimed that the next day, when he noticed that you hadn't made it, he'd threatened to quit and take the news public himself. At that point, he said, he convinced you to do the right thing. Only he hadn't known that you'd been selling your shares the day before. "I couldn't believe it," he told *Time* magazine. "Here I was, thinking of the poor families that were soon going to find out that our faulty shirts had caused their kids' deaths, and there he was, trying to keep count of his millions. Just disgusting."

You are spared a prison sentence, however, because the government ultimately fails to prove Barry's assertion that he had told you about the T-shirt failures on Thursday afternoon. The board of Fleece, of course, had a lower burden of proof, and they didn't believe a word you said.

In an act of charity, Barry—the new CEO of Fleece—allowed you to take ownership from Fleece of the brand Harry. ("Why would we want to promote the brand of an obvious criminal?" he asked you while signing the papers in your old office.) You even convince Araz and Jeff to come with you and start an edgier, urban line of clothes that evoke a sense of danger and malice. The new company, Hard Harry, is a modest success—nothing like Fleece in its heyday, of course, but you manage to make a few media lists of disgraced CEOs who climb back into respectability.

You decide, in the end, that it would be a bad idea to take Hard Harry public.

The end

It's one year later and you're lying on the bed of room 318. Diane is not there. In fact, you haven't heard from her since that phone call. . . . But your wife did. She received a letter from Diane a week after the call—one sentence written on the Pierre's stationery that read: "I've been fucking your husband for two years." Signed, simply, "Diane."

You had a lot of explaining to do—none of it very effective. Diane also sent a picture of you to the *New York Post*. You're wearing her yellow panties and a Red Sox hat, and you're hand-cuffed to the minibar of room 318, drunk on Patron. Your divorce is ugly. Your family is destroyed. Apple is the star in the most downloaded sex movie in the history of the Internet. Apparently the short film she was making for class turned out to be a two-hour sex romp with the entire bull pen of the New York Mets.

Your wife divorced you and got half of everything, including your stock in Fleece, putting you in a minority position on the board of your own company. She then built a coalition of some of the board members and had you booted out of the company. You now live off the licensing fees of Silk Armor and have a new mix of friends that you met hiking at Bear Mountain.

Your eyes wander from the oil painting of the mallards flying over a canoe down to the Egyptian monkey with enormous balls on your $15,000 umbrella stand.

You ponder selling the thing on eBay and taking a trip to Tibet to climb Everest. But then you decide to take a nap.

The end

Baldacker walks into your office wearing an Argonauts jersey over his suit.

"Cute, Alan. Very cute. How's business been while I've been out there on the gridiron with all my new friends?"

"Sales are continuing to explode," he replies. "We're selling those Homer jerseys for a hundred and twenty-five dollars a pop and they only cost us about fifteen bucks to make."

"Excellent," you say. "That's all part of the plan. Although, remember, it's not Fleece that owns this team. The company will make some extra dinars by selling those jerseys, but if I can start selling out this stadium again, all that money is going into my own pocket."

Baldacker frowns very briefly and shuffles a few papers in his lap.

"What? What's the problem, Alan? Fleece didn't borrow the money to buy the Corporals—I did. We sell some jerseys, great. But it's my ass that's on the line here."

"Actually, boss, no it's not. When we were private, you could borrow whatever you wanted on the Fleece credit line, and no one cared—you owned the whole company. But now that we're public, we can't really just gloss over the fact that Fleece is guaranteeing six hundred and ten million of your loans. We need to account for that in our next financial filing, which is due next week. Nothing in our IPO prospectus said that we were going to go into the business of guaranteeing loans so that you could go out and buy a sports team."

"What? This has nothing to do with Fleece! It's my money," you say. "Just because the company is guaranteeing the loans doesn't mean they'll ever have to pay for them!"

"True, but you've still put a possible six-hundred-and-ten-million-dollar liability on the company's books. I should remind you, if you don't mind my saying so, that now that Fleece is public, there's a board of directors to answer to. They'll replace you if they find that you've been putting your own interests ahead of the company's."

He's right. You took a gamble with your company's money—with shareholders' money. How could you be so blind? You can't bear the idea of the board firing you from the company you started, but on the other hand, are you prepared to engage in fraud? You *could* just tell him to keep the debt off the company's books.

15 ↑1.75 ADLAC 22 ↓2.60 ENE 50.50 ↑1.50 TYC 60.25 ↓1.75 MSO 65 ↑2.

Do you tell your CFO to keep the debt off Fleece's books? Go to page 27.
Or do you come clean and face the board's judgment on your decision?
Go to page 183.

Before Flaxworthy can say anything, you blurt out, "Jerry, we have to talk. There's something I didn't tell you just now."

For the second time today Flaxworthy just stares back at you without saying anything.

"I don't know who you were just talking to in there, but I think I can guess. Fleece has a big problem," you say. "Just this morning we discovered that one of our accountants has been rigging the books for years. As far as I can tell, we're going to need to restate all our financials going back to the early nineties. I know I should have told you this first thing, but I just found out myself and I've pretty much been in shock since."

Flaxworthy doesn't seem surprised. Actually, he just looks battle weary, as if he's heard it all before. "Is everyone corrupt?" he asks in a deadpan voice, leading you back into your own conference room with the air of a repo man about to commandeer a Cadillac.

"You know, DAs are building their careers nosing through accounting books these days. They're stringing people up for stealing paper clips. If what you're saying is true, we've got a case of fraud on our hands. Someone will go to jail for this."

"Me?" is all you can say. "But I didn't know anything. I just told you, I only found out this morning."

"No, not you necessarily," he says. "But somebody."

"Weiss!" you say without thinking.

"Who?"

"Weiss is our accountant," you explain. "He's the one who hid one-point-five billion dollars. I don't even know how he did it. What I do know, however, is that he's sitting in my office as we speak and is quite unnerved by it all. I gather he should be."

"Damn right he should," says Flaxworthy. "Has he admitted to it?"

"Well, here's the thing," you say. "Our counsel . . . Barry . . . I just came from a meeting with him and J. P. Moneyhouse during which they tried to get me to cover this all up."

Flaxworthy's eyes light up. "Moneyhouse? He's involved?"

"As of this morning, yes, although I don't know how much he knows," you say.

Flaxworthy is clearly distracted. If you didn't know any better, you'd think he was imagining his face on the cover of *Fortune* or *Business Week*: THE MAN WHO BROUGHT DOWN MONEYHOUSE'S HOUSE OF CARDS.

"Okay," he says, snapping back to reality. "We need to get your man Weiss right now and find out how much Moneyhouse knows. Weiss is small-time. We've been looking for a way to get at Moneyhouse for years. This is perfect. It could bring down Moneyhouse and Stonecutter for good."

"Well, as I said, he's in my office. Let's go have a chat with him."

E 15 ↑1.75 ADLAC 22 ↓2.60 ENE 50.50 ↑1.50 TYC 60.25 ↓1.75 MSO 65 ↑2.

Go to page 100.

Jennifer Estrangelo enters your office seemingly unaware that anything could be wrong. She even hands you some Girl Scout cookies.

"I know you love Thin Mints," she says, standing the box upright on your desk before sitting herself down in the chair across from you, chomping on a Thin Mint herself.

Estrangelo's confidence is unshakable. She must know that she is in a world of shit, but you'd never know it from her demeanor. That is why she is the head of sales and that is why you are bracing yourself for a big, drawn-out fight.

"Jennifer, can you explain to me why complete shipments of our stretch workout gear are arriving at our Newark warehouse as returns?"

Jennifer pops another cookie into her mouth. "News to me," she says with apparent disinterest. You look at her, knowing that she's not going to take the bait of your seemingly honest question.

"It shouldn't be news to you, because, according to Donny, you authorized the loading of trucks packed with product with absolutely no destination except to another one of our warehouses to be labeled as returns!"

"I'm in sales—I don't deal in returns. And if you're accusing me of some sort of fraud, you better get some proof before I get my lawyer in here and sue your bulletproof pants off for character assassination."

15 ↑1.75 ADLAC 22 ↓ 2.60 ENE 50.50 ↑ 1.50 TYC 60.25 ↓ 1.75 MSO 65 ↑ 2.50

Go to page 60.

The reactions to your decision to end your marriage for a younger woman vary along fairly predictable lines.

Your wife has disappeared. When you told her, she stared back at you and said, "You bastard," and then turned and walked out of the apartment. You haven't seen her since, and Apple has steadfastly maintained that she hasn't heard from her.

Apple pretends not to care, but it pains you to see how much you've actually wounded her. When you're not with Sally, you're at home with Apple making TV dinners and trying to ignore the fact that you have too much to say to each other to say anything at all. Even when you do speak, Apple can't talk to you for more than a few seconds, or tears start to well up in her eyes. Your heart is filled and hers is broken.

The press, on the other hand, obviously cares quite a bit. While a few moralist columnists condemn you for abandoning your wife, most writers see it as rejuvenation for Fleece—and for your increasingly tabloid-friendly personal life. There's no such thing as bad press.

But what do you care what people think? This has nothing to do with your business, and it has nothing to do with how effectively you can run a business. This is about romance. This is about new beginnings. This is about mind-blowing sex.

The kind you used to have with Fawn. She, not surprisingly, is shattered. During the on-and-off affair you've been having with her for years, you'd convinced her that if you ever left your wife, it would be for her. She quits the day after you make your announcement. No notice. No good-bye.

15 ↑1.75 ADLAC 22 ↓2.60 ENE 50.50 ↑1.50 TYC 60.25 ↓1.75 MSO 65 ↑2.

Go to page 46.

You grab your phone and call Barry back into your office.

"I was just about to sell my shares," you say with tremendous relief.

"Yeah, I was thinking of doing it too," he says, smiling sheepishly.

"It's crazy, right? The richer we get, the weaker we get. But you know what? We're stronger than that—Fleece clothing is stronger than that. We have to be as strong and resilient as the Silk Armor we make!"

He nods, and the two of you sit in silence for a few moments.

"We have to tell the staff so they're ready when the news hits," you continue. "I can't understand how it happened. I fired guns at those shirts myself, from a lot closer than fifty yards, and the bullets were bouncing off of the things."

"I don't know what to say, boss," he says.

"This is terrible, Barry. Everything we worked for, ruined because of one faulty T-shirt. All right, let's call the staff into the conference room and break the news. Tell Fawn to call the deli downstairs and order up a couple of cases of beer. We're going to need it."

You gather everyone into the conference room. The room is packed, standing room only as you give your best battle speech.

"I have terrible news. A soldier by the name of Pat Mayhew was killed today in Iraq—a sad end to a young life. None of you knew this man, but he was wearing a Silk Armor T-shirt and a bullet went right through it. When news of this death hits the street, our stock will take a tremendous hit. This could be the end of Fleece as we know it. But if we are marked to die, so be it. If we survive this terrible turn of events, we will be stronger for it. I don't wish for money anymore, or wish that the world wears Fleece. All I want now is for the company to survive— and then succeed again. But I cannot do it alone. I need all of you. I look forward to seeing you all tomorrow morning, on a new day full of new opportunities. Enjoy the beer."

You leave the shell-shocked staff in the conference room. The only sound is that of the interns opening the first beers. Now you have to break the news to your wife.

15 ↑1.75 ADLAC 22 ↓2.60 ENE 50.50 ↑1.50 TYC 60.25 ↓1.75 MSO 65 ↑2.

Go to page 32.

"Here's what you're going to do, Baldacker," you say to your CFO. "First, you're going to pretend this conversation never happened. And second, you're not going to put that six hundred and ten million on our books. Understood?"

Baldacker sits, staring at you, waiting for you to break into laughter so he can laugh too. You don't laugh. You don't even blink. You stare your CFO down to see if he flinches.

He does.

"Sir, with all due respect, I can't engage in this sort of thing."

"Okay, Alan. If you can't do this, I will find someone who can. You see, it's not that big a deal. Reporting this debt will only hurt the stock . . . and your reputation as a competent CFO."

Baldacker stands and nods at you before leaving your office. *He will come to see that this is the right thing to do,* you think as you turn your attention back to the small triangle of paper that you flick with your fingers over your lamp and into the trash can. "Field goal! The Argonauts squeak by with a Super Bowl victory!"

A few days later you get a draft of the quarterly report, and it appears that Baldacker has followed orders flawlessly. *He's a team player,* you think as you stuff it into your Argonauts gym bag, which has replaced your briefcase, and rush off to check out practice at Swamplands.

The team treats you a lot better than the first time you met them. No laughing, no pointing, but rather handshakes and the occasional, "Hey, Captain"—a nickname they've given you since their rout of the Grizzlies.

At the end of practice, the players once again pour Gatorade on you. "I'm going to get pneumonia if you guys keep doing this!"

"It's a tradition now," says Red. "They did it before last week's game and they won. They'll keep doing it until they lose."

"We won't ever lose again!" shouts your four-hundred-pound defensive tackle, nicknamed the Hummer.

"Captain, what are you doing tonight? Making bulletproof socks?" asks Homer.

"Dinner at home, I think."

"Why don't you come out to Scores with us for the Hummer's birthday?" he says, throwing a towel at you.

Scores? The most exclusive strip club in New York? Believe it or not, you've never been there and have always wanted to check it out. And going with a professional football team? You'll be treated like royalty.

"All right. I'm in!"

You wake up the next morning with the kind of hangover that you haven't had since your frat house days. You can barely open your eyes and your head feels like it's filled with hot cement. It's 10:30 in the morning. Your wife has left for the day, and you don't blame her. You smell like a White Russian served in an ashtray. You're late for work but you don't care. You are in serious pain.

You turn on the TV to check on Fleece's stock. Your quarterly report was filed today, so you watch the scroll to see how it's doing, even though the streaming symbols give you motion sickness.

The stock is doing well. Investors were happy with the report, and apparently the company's connection to the Argonauts has turned it into a "trendy" investment to boot. Good for now.

While showering, the evening comes back to you in pieces as the hot water pounds out the pain. Kamikaze shots, a lap dance by an Asian woman named Crystal, the VIP room, the cast from *Oceans Twelve*, a lap dance by a blond woman named Crystal, champagne, singing into a beer bottle, and finally, a lap dance from a busty redhead named Crystal.

You get out of the shower and you're feeling a little better—enough to turn up the sound on the TV to watch Claire Illustrado, the "Money Bunny," report from the floor of the exchange. You're not really listening to her until you hear: "Trading in Fleece stock has been halted by the New York Stock Exchange as a result of an overwhelming number of sell orders. While investors were quite happy with Fleece's own filing, the mood changed after they caught wind of the quarterly report of TownGroup. Apparently the global bank reported an outstanding loan of six hundred and ten million dollars to the CEO of Fleece that was guaranteed by Fleece itself—but was not included in Fleece's own filing. Before the halt Fleece shares were down more than fifty percent."

Your hangover worsens as you try to get dressed as quickly as possible. You rush out of your building and into a waiting cab. You barely survive the slalomlike driving of your taxi without puking from the hangover and the bad news. When you get to your office building and pull out your wallet to pay the driver, you see your credit card receipt from Scores: $129,626.00.

5 ↑ 1.75 ADLAC 22 ↓ 2.60 ENE 50.50 ↑ 1.50 TYC 60.25 ↓ 1.75 MSO 65 ↑ 2.50

Go to page 120.

The next morning you drive Tiffany to Century City and kiss her on the forehead, wishing her good luck and saying good-bye, as you are hopping on a plane back east this afternoon. You think you might be falling in love with this blond siren, the kind of love that a teenager has, the kind that is unrelenting, unreasonable, and unquenchable.

You show up on the Fox lot to meet with Stu Kovacs. Stu is short and squat with absolutely no hair on his body. Rumor has it that when his $170 million futuristic epic *Water Planet* pulled in a meager $200,000 in its two weeks in the theaters, he lost all his body hair the night he had to make the decision to pull it from the screens.

You are sunk deep in a black leather couch in Stu's waiting room. His secretary, a tall, willowy has-been model with a short brown bob, is clipping articles from *Variety*. As far as she's concerned, you're not even there. You think, *I'm a goddamn CEO! How can he keep me waiting for twenty minutes? Isn't there some unwritten code of ethics among leaders of industry that keeps us from making one another feel like jackasses?*

Stu finally enters the waiting room sucking down a protein beet shake. He throws a large padded envelope on his secretary's desk, startling her and sending *Variety* clippings all over the room.

"It's a cowboy script from Ted Danson. Open it, read it, and let me know if I should burn it." Stu is all business and doesn't care that he has flustered his secretary. You try to stand up from the couch but are so deeply implanted in its cushions that it takes some maneuvering. It seems that only the squeaking noise of your struggle to get up is what finally alerts Stu to your presence. He turns toward you, motions to the door of his office, and walks in without saying a word.

E 15 ↑1.75 ADLAC 22 ↓2.60 ENE 50.50 ↑1.50 TYC 60.25 ↓1.75 MSO 65 ↑2.

Go to page 184.

Twelve months later you're still the CEO of Fleece. But it's a private company now. You took Carlucci's advice and launched an offer for all of the outstanding shares the day after your analyst meeting. Investors fell all over themselves trying to sell them back to you. Dickens kicked in $15 million of his own, and the rest came from you, Araz, Jeff, Baldacker, and your in-house lawyer, Barry.

Sales have rebounded, profits are up, and Fleece is once again in the headlines. But it's for a much different reason this time.

While you do reinvest some of the company's profits in R & D and marketing, you now donate at least 50 percent of earnings to environmental, veteran, and educational causes. You use only textiles that have been grown without pesticides, and you have given tear-away clothing to all of the disabled Iraq war veterans.

Your company's new motto is "Don't Be So Evil," and you restrict management salaries to a maximum of six times the compensation of the lowliest employees. And you were *Time* magazine's Man of the Year last year. The cover line: HARRY HELPS. Phowl, the most popular jam band in the country, even wrote a song about the company called "Silk Amour."

You've returned to the ideals and values that helped create Fleece in the first place. And Apple never even needed to change schools.

The end

Your wife goes through a cycle of disbelief, anger, crying, resolve, and then anger again. Despite all of your claims to the contrary, she puts the impending failure of Fleece squarely on your shoulders and insists that you sleep on the couch.

The next morning you choose your wardrobe carefully. You are sure that as soon as the government announces the failure of Fleece shirts, the news media will be banging on the company's doors. So you have to look good. You put on your best purple shirt, a navy suit, and a tie that Apple gave you for your fiftieth birthday.

On the way to the office you call the local precinct and explain to the staff sergeant that there might be some commotion at the Fleece offices in the afternoon, and you ask if they would mind sending over a couple of uniformed officers. They agree to do so, and the cops are waiting outside your office when you arrive.

The next several hours are excruciating. You watch CNN for an hour or so, waiting for an announcement, but it never airs. You notice, however, that Fleece stock is trending steadily downward. Perhaps someone has leaked the news in Washington.

To distract yourself, you invite the police to watch your promotional DVD that shows your lab technicians taking turns firing an AK-47 at a test mannequin that's made of iron and is dressed in one of Fleece's new camouflage tank tops.

"Have you guys talked to the NYPD about making some of these for us?" one asks, after watching the shirt deflect everything thrown at it.

"No, we haven't. But that's a good idea," you say. *It would have been,* you think, *if we weren't going out of business today. And if the shirts actually worked.*

At 4:00 your phone rings. Fawn tells you it's someone from the Securities and Exchange Commission. They're calling about rampant selling of Fleece shares by employees, and they want to know if there's anything they should know about. "Not that I know of," you say, "but I'll look into it." When you hang up the phone you're even more depressed. Even those you trusted are abandoning ship.

In the end, they shouldn't have. At 6:00 Barry gets a phone call from his mysterious government contact, who tells him that it had all been a mistake, and that the soldier who'd been shot wasn't wearing a Fleece shirt after all. Instead, he'd been wearing a homemade T-shirt that said, GIVE PEACE A CHANCE. Now they want *every* soldier wearing Fleece. And they've doubled their current orders.

It's not all sunshine and laughter, though. You are forced to fire about fifty employees, each of whom had sold all of their Fleece shares in anticipation of the government's announcement. While they are never charged with insider trading since the "inside information" proved nonexistent, you are merciless in telling them that they betrayed your trust and that of their colleagues.

Word ultimately leaks out to the press, and your star rises even higher than before. You are characterized as the CEO who held strong in the face of impending disaster, without resorting to dumping your shares or handing the steering wheel to someone else as you slip into early retirement. Your wife even apologizes for not believing in you.

The next season, Fleece debuts its "Fleece Fuzz" line of bulletproof clothing for police officers. It's an instant hit. You hire the two cops—the ones who had originally made the suggestion—to run Fleece's security. They also run weekly target practice sessions for the guards in the product testing lab, killing two birds with one stone.

The end

That afternoon you decide to leave the office early. You grab your coat and shut down your computer. As you're heading to your office door, you glance at the Sven Spiegel painting of a downhill skier wearing a Silk Armor skin suit. Spiegel himself signed it: "To the man whose designs make my paintings masterpieces." You wonder whether you should take it down. What if the Feds come here and ask about that? You didn't pay tax on it, either. Then you think of Sutinis again. She said she'd take care of it, and whenever she's said that in the past, she was true to her word. You decide to leave it where it hangs and figure you might as well try to get Fawn to agree to a quick tryst at the Sheraton across the street.

Fawn is busily typing at her computer and trying to keep a straight face as you sit on the corner of her desk, dazzling her with ideas of elaborate locations for a possible afternoon quickie.

"Bethesda fountain, the roof of the Plaza, the Columbus Circle subway platform, the Staten Island Ferry men's room . . ."

"You're dirty," Fawn giggles, keeping her eyes fixed on her spreadsheet.

Just then two men in trench coats walk around the corner. "Are you the CEO of Fleece?" one says, looking as serious as John Ashcroft. The other just stares at Fawn's blouse.

Fawn pipes up, "Who, may I ask, is wondering?"

"The FBI," says the unshaven heavyset one, still staring at Fawn's breasts.

"That would be me," you say, trying to be as congenial as possible and to put on a front that suggests there can be no good reason why the FBI would be at your office.

You follow the first agent's gaze into your office and all you can think is, *Sven Spiegel! Sven Spiegel!*

"I think we will be comfortable in the conference room," you say as you jump off Fawn's desk. You start walking down the hall with the two agents following you. You open the door to the conference room and let the agents in first. And to your dismay you see Sutinis's "Marilyns" painting hanging on the opposite wall. The taller, clean-cut agent begins to take notes and the heavyset one pulls out a digital camera and photographs the painting.

Without looking at you, the heavyset agent says, "You better call your lawyer."

You nod, looking up at the Warhol painting and wondering how it got from Sutinis's office into the conference room.

15 ↑ 1.75 ADLAC 22 ↓ 2.60 ENE 50.50 ↑ 1.50 TYC 60.25 ↓ 1.75 MSO 65 ↑ 2.5

Go to page 226.

You decide to give Stubby a ring. Maybe he's in New York and wants to hit a Yankees playoff game. Maybe he has some of the girls from his last video with him. You dial his number.

"Yo! CEO! You may be chairman of the board, but never forget who's chairman of the boards!" Tyree is laughing the whole time he's saying this to you. He's obviously been smoking the chronic.

"What's going on, dog?" you ask, knowing that as hard as you try, you can never be cool.

"'Dog'? Who are you, Randy Jackson? Listen, get your ass to the West Coast. We have got to party. It's my thirtieth birthday on Saturday, and I'm having everybody come to my crib and party in my infinity pool!"

"I don't know if I can get away. I just went public two hours ago. I can't just get on a plane and party in LA."

"Do you like me wearing your shit? Do you like that the kids are wearing your shit because I wear your shit? If your answer to these questions is 'yes,' then fly your white ass to LAX and we're going to party."

"Okay, you've convinced me. I'll work it out and I'll see you this weekend."

You hang up. Bad timing for a party, but Tyree Stubbs *is* one of your biggest clients—and it'll definitely be fun. Maybe you can set up some meetings with a couple of studio heads about product placement to make the trip worthwhile.

You remember that you're due in a sales meeting in a few minutes and head down to the conference room. A dozen or so junior employees are sitting around the table, along with Jennifer Estrangelo, your head of sales.

You decide to open with a joke. "I hope you people can sell as many clothes as we've sold shares! Remember, we're a clothing company."

After some polite but unenthusiastic laughter, you get down to business. The one surprise of the meeting is when Estrangelo tells you that there has been overwhelming demand for Fleece's line of stretch workout gear ("for the weekend cross-trainer"). She thinks it would be prudent to place a massive order of the materials today so that you don't run into any supply problems. Any hiccups in sales in the next few months could spook the stock market.

"What do you mean by massive, Jennifer?" you ask.

"About fifty million dollars' worth," she says. She's not joking.

You're stunned. For one, you didn't think the line was selling well. Second, Estrangelo's bonus is going to be huge this year.

"Fine," you say as you walk out of the conference room. "Place the order."

The rest of your week is surprisingly uneventful. The only complicated negotiation you entered into was trying to convince your wife not to come to LA with you. The two of you are sitting in the living room of your duplex apartment on Riverside Drive.

"It's getting cold here in New York," she says. "I want a blast of sunshine. I need a base before we go to St. Bart's. You know how I hate tanning salons. The staff at those places can be so indiscreet."

"Baby, I'd love it if you could come, but I'm going to be so busy. Anyway, LA is only fun if you're a movie star. For everyone else it's boring."

You get your wife to agree by surprising her with a classic Cartier Tank watch. Your flight to LA is smooth. The only excitement in the five-hour trip is what's going on in your imagination. You constantly create elaborate mile-high fantasies about yourself and the stunning blond woman sitting immediately to your left. She's gorgeous and refuses to acknowledge your presence. Being ignored drives you wild. As the plane lands, you both get up, and you decide this is your last chance to break the ice.

"I hope you enjoy your stay in LA," you say, imitating the nasally flight attendant.

She looks at you and hands you the blanket that had been covering her tanned legs. She then walks off the plane without looking back. You hope the rest of your trip in California isn't so chilly.

Three hours later a chiseled would-be actor is handing you your third mojito on Stubby's back patio. You've got quite a buzz on. Tyree introduces you to TGIF, "The Gangsta in Full," who wants you to make him a Silk Armor bulletproof vest. You're too drunk to bother to explain to him that Silk Armor is already bulletproof and agree to get your designers "right on it" on Monday morning.

By midnight you think it's time to go. You want to be somewhat conscious when you drive through the Hollywood Hills back to your hotel. You say good-bye and are just about to open Tyree's glass sliding door when you find yourself face-to-face with the blond woman from the plane.

Go to page 50.

Diane is everything a man could ever want in a mistress. Olive skin that stretches over a fit body, and a mane of dirty blond hair that she wears like a crown of feminine prowess. She communicates only in whispers and possesses a dirty sense of humor, a love of scotch, and a fear of commitment.

You pick up your phone and call her. You get her voice mail. "Honey," you coo into the phone. "I just made two hundred mil. What do you say we meet in three eighteen?" What you're referring to, of course, is Room 318 at the Pierre, which you've been renting for the past five years. Diane is only its latest occupant.

You tell Fawn you've got to go to the garment district and look at some zippers, and you head for the elevator, putting on a Fleece baseball cap as you go.

Your cell phone rings and you see from the caller ID display that it's Diane: She's listed under "Mexican food."

"Where are you?" you ask her.

"I just woke up," she says. "I'm still at the Pierre."

"Well, stay there," you reply. "We've got some celebrating to do. Make sure you've got the blindfold and the chocolate sauce ready."

You walk outside and stroll over to the hotel. The wind is picking up, blowing tourists and their shopping bags full of Takashimaya swag across the sidewalk. But it doesn't slow you down. Not even the wind can catch you today.

As you round the corner onto Fifth, you tug on your baseball cap and head into the Pierre. The doorman, Serge, nods at you. He knows your game. But five thousand dollars every Christmas keeps him mum.

15 ↑1.75 ADLAC 22 ↓ 2.60 ENE 50.50 ↑1.50 TYC 60.25 ↓ 1.75 MSO 65 ↑ 2.50

Go to page 42.

TRANSCRIPT FOR PUBLIC RECORD:

UNITED STATES DISTRICT COURT. SOUTHERN DISTRICT OF NEW YORK

U.S.   ——————————

v.

DEFENDANT.   ——————————

FILED

CHARGES: Tax evasion, corporate fraud, grand larceny, wire fraud, interstate trafficking

BEATRICE SUTINIS: I was brought in to straighten out a company that was not ready to be public. Their books were a mess. Apparently they had invented crib sheets to cover up personal expenses. The likes of this kind of corruption is beyond the reaches of my imagination. I knew something was horribly wrong and that's why I had to blow the whistle.

J.P. MONEYHOUSE: A man like this CEO on trial is a vile man. A man who drags all of us who have made Wall Street a place of integrity into the mud of graft. My father would be turning over in his grave if he hadn't been cremated and sprinkled over the eighteenth green at Augusta.

CARSON RODRIGUEZ: He's the one who told me about the tax scam. I'm a designer. I know about tacky lapels, but I don't know any- thing about tax loopholes.

LARRY WEISS: I only did what I was told. The things he told me to do were . . . well, he's just a great salesman. I didn't think I was committing any crimes. I thought I was saving the company.

FAWN CORRIDOIR (ALSO SUING DEFENDANT FOR SEXUAL HARASSMENT): Being his personal secretary was a living hell. The day that the FBI agents came in to arrest him, he told me that I would have to have sex with him on the Staten Island Ferry or he would fire me. I'm a good woman and an excellent typist.

JOHNNY CONRAN: Just because this case is all about art doesn't mean you need to frame my client because you're in the mood to frame something . . . May I ask for a recess now? I have to tape my talk show.

15 ↑1.75 ADLAC 22 ↓2.60 ENE 50.50 ↑1.50 TYC 60.25 ↓1.75 MSO 65 ↑2.5

Go to page 89.

You are on Mt. Olympus with Apple, having hiked almost all the way to the peak. You are using this time to share some wisdom with your daughter. "When in doubt, always tell the truth, but if you're caught in a lie, keep lying. . . . Never buy clothes for the size you want to be; buy for the size you are. . . . Wake up at dawn at least once a year, and if you can't do that, at least stay up until dawn. . . . Look at that bird! It's too dumb to know it's beautiful; learn from that bird."

"Dad, you're a doofus. I wish you had let me bring my iPod."

You want to climb the last few hundred yards to take in the view of the great Pacific Northwest, but Apple is too exhausted.

"Come on, girl. We've made it this far. We only have a few more feet to go."

"We have like a thousand feet to go, and I'm exhausted! Jeez, Dad, I mean, can't you just look at the view from here?"

"Fine, I'll come back for you," you say.

"Fine. I hope you get eaten by a cougar."

You think you hear your name but conclude that you imagined it. It was a man's voice, and Apple is the only other person anywhere near you. You look back at her, though, and she seems to have heard it as well. You hear it again, and you look down the mountain to see a park ranger walking up the trail at a brisk pace.

"Did you call my name?" you ask.

"Yes. Please, you and your daughter have to come down. There's been an accident."

"Is it my wife?"

"No. Jason Homer drove his truck into a lake. Apparently he was racing another teammate."

"This must be a joke."

"I assure you it's not."

"Oh my God. Let's go, Apple."

"Thank God."

15 ↑ 1.75 ADLAC 22 ↓ 2.60 ENE 50.50 ↑ 1.50 TYC 60.25 ↓ 1.75 MSO 65 ↑ 2.5

Go to page 191.

You've barely started knocking when the door of 318 opens. Diane puts a blindfold on you, shoves you toward the bed, and pulls your pants down. You smell chocolate on her breath. You climax before your pants hit your ankles.

"You son of a bitch," she says half-jokingly, pulling the blindfold off you. "That landed in my hair. What about me?"

"Baby, I'm sorry," you say. "I'm just amped up about this new investment opportunity we're working on at Fleece. You won't believe this, but we're getting involved in Nigerian barges."

"I love it when you talk money," she purrs. "Where's Nigeria? In Asia?"

"Africa, sweetheart. Africa," you reply. "Hey, wait! Didn't you just inherit four hundred thousand from your grandfather? Put it in this thing and you'll see a five hundred percent return. Guaranteed."

"But that's all the savings I have," she says. "I'm supposed to put it all in one investment? How do you know I won't lose it all?"

"It's guaranteed. I'm not just thinking about your future, baby. I'm thinking about *our* future. As soon as this IPO stuff is all taken care of, I'm going to make it official. I'm getting a divorce. From here on in, three eighteen is only going to be the place we stay when we're not in our villa on Lake Como, rubbing nipples with George Clooney."

She shivers for a second and falls back on the bed. "Jesus Christ. I just came myself."

15 ↑1.75 ADLAC 22 ↓2.60 ENE 50.50 ↑1.50 TYC 60.25 ↓1.75 MSO 65 ↑2.5

Go to page 129.

"Thanks very much for the call, Mr. Sippowicz. This is the kind of opportunity that only comes along once in a lifetime—or every time we go to war, ha-ha—but because it would require a retooling of our entire production process, I really should check with my board first."

He doesn't laugh at your joke. "That's fair," he says. "But don't shilly-shally on this. The offer won't be around forever." And then he hangs up.

Shilly-shally? Who the hell says "shilly-shally"? you think. *Washington. Bunch of wackos.*

Still, it's something you should seriously consider. You call Araz and Jeff into your office and tell them about the call. They are both resolute in their opposition to the idea.

"We don't make *T-shirts*!" says Araz. "Hanes makes T-shirts! Fruit of the Loom makes T-shirts! We make Silk Armor!"

"Listen to what you're saying, Araz," you reply. "Silk *Armor*. We make *armor*. That's what soldiers need. And it would be a PR coup if we announced that we're making it safer for America's youth on the ground in Iraq."

"A PR coup?" he responds. "This war is the worst PR disaster this country has ever seen. And I will not take any part in it. I never thought I'd say this, but if you decide to do this deal, I will submit my resignation."

"Same here," says Jeff. The two of them stare at you, waiting for your response. The bastards. They know you know how much of Fleece's success is a result of their particular magic. Sure, you could triple sales this year, but without Araz and Jeff, what would you possibly do to follow up?

"Fine. You win. We won't do it. We'll stick to our knitting, as they say. Now get out of my office. I've got work to do."

15 ↑ 1.75 ADLAC 22 ↓ 2.60 ENE 50.50 ↑ 1.50 TYC 60.25 ↓ 1.75 MSO 65 ↑ 2.5

Go to page 48.

"God, you make me feel alive!" you tell Sally. "Like I can do anything. You are truly a remarkable woman. My wife is so afraid of taking risks. It's like living with an albatross around my neck."

You know that a divorce will cost you half of your fortune, but you can certainly live quite well on what's left. Plus there are the perks that the board of Fleece has set up for you even after your retirement. But all the money in the world can't buy this kind of happiness—this kind of satisfaction.

Less than an hour later you're holding hands in the backseat of your helicopter, flying over Westport. You realize that soon you will have to part ways. How are you going to tell your wife? You brace yourself for what you think will be an all-out, tear-down brawl with her. Your wife has been at your side through it all and this is how you repay her? By leaving her? It's not right. It's not reasonable, but then again, who ever said love was reasonable?

"I'd love a house by the water," says Laufetter.

"Consider it done," you say as you look out the window at the mansions below.

15 ↑1.75 ADLAC 22 ↓2.60 ENE 50.50 ↑1.50 TYC 60.25 ↓1.75 MSO 65 ↑2.5

Go to page 24.

The next twelve months are a blur. You never realized how cheap it is to live in New York when someone else is paying your way. You were hesitant about Carson Rodriguez decorating your house at first, but he actually did a really tasteful job and never touched a thing in your den.

With all the money you've been saving by having Fleece cover every imaginable expense, you've even taken up a new hobby: art collecting. Carson has great connections in the art world, and you've got him jet-setting around the globe making purchases for you. Your house is a veritable gallery: Basquiat, Haring, Warhol, Klee, and a Kostabi for Apple.

Carson has even brought you in on a little tax loophole he knows about. Even though you're buying the art for your New York apartment, you have all the paintings shipped to a warehouse in New Hampshire to avoid paying taxes. It's funny that a designer is teaching you about high finance.

Sutinis has worked out great as well. She's covered your ass on the accounting front and has even turned out to be a pretty good friend. You and she play squash together several times a week, and you've gotten her to quit smoking by convincing her that the smoke gives her away when she eavesdrops.

15 ↑1.75 ADLAC 22 ↓2.60 ENE 50.50 ↑1.50 TYC 60.25 ↓1.75 MSO 65 ↑2.50

Go to page 240.

You start looking for a new secretary immediately. *This time*, you think, *I'm going to find a more homely assistant to avoid the temptation.* You end up hiring Mabel Lubner, a sixty-five-year-old Queens native with a permanent limp and a mole with hairs growing out of it on her left cheek. The change is so transparent that everyone in the office concludes that you really might be in love with Laufetter. (They all knew about you and Fawn. . . . They always do.)

You and Sally both have to pay the price for your relationship. At the *Ivy Business Review* the bookish staff considers the affair a breach of journalistic ethics, especially since Laufetter had let you edit your own profile. They also blame Laufetter for smearing their glowing reputation with a sex scandal—despite the fact that no one in the country even reads the publication. Sally is forced to resign as editor of the review. You are all she has now, and she wants to get married.

You repeatedly explain to Laufetter that you want to get a divorce from your wife, but that you still haven't heard a word from her and have no idea where she is. Apple has passed along a message that she is okay, but that's all she's told you to date.

Araz and Jeff are pleading with you to get divorced as well, as they love the idea of the face of Harry being single. You've told them that you plan to marry Laufetter, but they don't want to hear it.

In the meantime business at Fleece is going well. Laufetter has been a fount of new ideas, including a lingerie line that fits comfortably underneath a woman's suit, with the tag line "Just because you're a woman of business doesn't mean you can't be a woman of pleasure." The two of you have made a habit of eating late dinners at your desk to avoid the paparazzi. You have yet to even entertain the notion of bringing Sally home for fear of traumatizing Apple.

Go to page 196.

Six months and hundreds of thousands of dollars later, you no longer recognize your apartment. Your den has been converted into a Zen rock garden with your favorite leather chair replaced by a wicker bench. The kitchen boulder replaced your fridge as promised, leaving room only for a small dorm fridge. And your bedroom now features an authentic Chinese opium bed that you need a step stool to climb in and out of. Sleeping on that bed is about as comfortable as sleeping at the bus station. No wonder people need to be on opium to enjoy the thing in the first place.

Who would ever think that so little comfort and so much noise could be so expensive? Nevertheless, it's made your wife happy, and Apple doesn't seem to mind because her room wasn't touched.

You've been getting most of your best sleeping in during the day in room 318 at the Pierre Hotel on a real bed, and you've been eating out with your family almost every night. Tonight the three of you are sitting in a banquette at Aix when the maître d' comes up to the table.

You hold your hand out to him, signaling for him to wait as you finish telling Apple a joke.

"What did the monkey say to the leopard at the card game?" you ask. She shrugs, stuffing a piece of garlic bread into her mouth. "I thought you were a cheetah. . . ."

"Sir, there's a phone call for you. Would you like to take it in the office? It's your doorman. He says it's an emergency."

15 ↑ 1.75 ADLAC 22 ↓ 2.60 ENE 50.50 ↑ 1.50 TYC 60.25 ↓ 1.75 MSO 65 ↑ 2.5

Go to page 166.

You leave a message with Sippowicz's secretary that you regret the decision, but Fleece will be unable to bid on the T-shirt contract.

You then call Carlucci to thank him for whatever role he played in the process, but also to tell him that you won't be bidding for the business. You hadn't quite anticipated the extent of his reaction.

"What? You did what? Oh my God. Kove is going to go ballistic. Shit, shit, shit. He's going to cut me out of the China deal."

You're confused. "What are you talking about, Fred? He offered me the opportunity to do some business with the government, and I politely declined. What does that have to do with you and the China deal?"

"Jesus, you New Yorkers have your heads up your asses," he says. "You think that you can make any decision with impunity, just because you have a Madison Avenue office and a pretty, blond wife."

"She's a brunette, Fred," you interrupt.

"That's not the point," he almost screams into the phone. "New York is not the center of the universe! Washington is. And when Kove dishes out favors, you take them. You don't 'politely decline' offers that are really coming from the president himself. Think about it: You just said no to the one man in the world that no one says no to!"

He's right. "Maybe it's not too late," you offer. "Maybe I can call Sippowicz back and tell him I want to do the deal. Araz and Jeff will quit, but that doesn't matter. . . ."

"Who the hell are Araz and Jeff? And don't be ridiculous. It *is* too late. If you think the president doesn't already know that you refused his generosity, then you're even dumber than you already appear to be. If I were you, I'd be making sure that Fleece is in compliance with every single government regulation you can think of, because the hammer is probably already falling toward you. Christ! This China deal was going to be huge. I've got to go. I've got to do my own damage control." Carlucci slams down his phone.

5 ↑ 1.75 ADLAC 22 ↓ 2.60 ENE 50.50 ↑ 1.50 TYC 60.25 ↓ 1.75 MSO 65 ↑ 2.50

Go to page 97.

The next morning you wake up to find the blond woman in your bed. Stephanie? No, Tiffany.

The rest of last night's party begins to take blurry shape in the back of your head before emerging as startling vignettes that are projected into your frontal lobe.

You: Opening the sliding door with an uncharacteristically well-developed opening line: "I hope you're a lot friendlier on the ground than you are in the air."

Her: After being told by Tyree that you're the wealthy CEO of Fleece, confessing that she has a fear of flying and she meant no offense. (You knew it was a lie, but you let her get away with it.)

Her again: Kneeling in front of Tyree's twelve-foot-long glass coffee table, snorting extraordinarily long lines of cocaine. ("That's so eighties," you said to her. "Baby, the eighties are back," she responded.)

Tyree: Screaming at you that he can't believe you're about to win a drunken game of H-O-R-S-E against the best basketball players on the West Coast.

Her: Laughing hysterically as you make a left turn at a red light onto Sunset Boulevard on your way back to the Chateau Marmont.

The two of you: Sweating through the sheets after a marathon session of drunken coitus.

You're staring at her naked body, wondering what this means for your marriage, when she opens her eyes.

"Good morning, flyboy," she says.

The next couple of days are a nonstop rush of activity. The early mornings you spend having breakfast meetings with various studio heads about getting Fleece's products in the movies. You meet with one of them, Moe Franklin, who is a throwback from an older era of B movies. This man is a survivor. He has thinning red hair that is spiked in the front and tied in a pony-tail in the back. He wears sunglasses indoors and his floral shirt is always open. He has an idea for a futuristic cop movie where the hero wears Silk Armor and brings justice to a postapocalyptic society. You tell him you'll finance a fifth of the cost if he can get the rest of the money. You know the deal's sour when he ducks out of the restaurant, leaving you with the check.

The afternoons are spent shopping with Tiffany. You spend most of your time waiting outside boutique dressing rooms as she tries on different outfits and dresses that she needs for auditions. Tiffany is an actress. Apparently she played a corpse on a *CSI: Cleveland* episode last season.

Your evenings are taken up with extravagant meals in over-hyped and overpriced restaurants, where you spend your time gazing at Tiffany's unbelievable body and she spends her time casing the place for people she can give her head shot to. But always you end up back at the Chateau Marmont making the beast with two backs.

You haven't even called your wife in the last two days. When she's called you, your response has been a consistent, "Baby, it's a bad time, I'm just about to walk into a meeting. I love you and we'll talk later."

Even though your time with Tiffany has made you feel young again (a cliché that holds true for any man in his fifties), you are feeling drawn back to New York City and your life there. You have one more meeting tomorrow and then you'll head back. You roll over in bed to look at Tiffany, who is going over a script for an audition tomorrow as an FBI agent on *The Sopranos*. You kiss her shoulder and tell her to break a leg. You've got a big day tomorrow too.

Go to page 30.

"Carson, I don't know what kind of trouble you've gotten your-self into, but I'll call you a lawyer. Which precinct is holding you?" you say, looking up at Araz and Jeff and noticing that their minds are working overtime trying to figure out what's going on.

"I'm not in trouble. *We're* in trouble, big boy. I'm in a hold-ing cell in Dover, New Hampshire. The feds busted the ware-house as I was picking up your Peter Max painting. You see, I pick up the paintings myself because that's the kind of service you're paying for. No one else will do that!"

"Shit, Carson." You look up at Araz and Jeff. They're frozen still, staring at you. You point to the door. "Guys, we'll finish this later." They frown simultaneously and reluctantly head to the door. You get out your pad to start keeping notes on the conversation. "Carson, you didn't tell them who you're getting the painting for, did you?"

"I didn't have to. Your name was on the crate. We're totally busted. You have to get me out of this cell. There's a man in a red checkered hunting jacket who won't let me sit down any-where."

"I can't believe this! I'm getting you a lawyer! And in the meantime I want you to keep your mouth shut, if that's at all possible!"

You pick up the phone and dial Sutinis.

"Hey, I'm in a meeting with Weiss, can I call you back?" she says into the speakerphone.

"Get me off speaker." She does. "Get in here now. I think we're in trouble."

Sutinis enters your office. She calmly shuts the door, sits on your sofa, and lights up a Dunhill.

"I thought you quit," you say, joining her on the couch.

"I did. What's the problem?"

You go into detail with Sutinis about how Carson was nabbed at the art warehouse. Sutinis is well aware of the scam.

After all, that's how she got the Warhol "Marilyns" painting in her office. You both commiserate about the idiocy of this interior designer and chain smoke her Dunhills until they're gone.

Sutinis gets up off the couch and throws the empty pack of cigarettes into the garbage can across the room. "Don't worry about this. I'll take care of it. I've dealt with worse."

She opens the door and walks out, giving you a wink as she closes the door. Damn, she's good.

5 ↑ 1.75 ADLAC 22 ↓ 2.60 ENE 50.50 ↑ 1.50 TYC 60.25 ↓ 1.75 MSO 65 ↑ 2.50

Go to page 34.

A voice comes through the other end of the line, sounding both hungover and angry. "What?"

"St. James? Is that you? Long time no talk."

"Who the fuck is this?"

"It's your old buddy from Fleece. I was very sorry to hear about the dismantling of your group. Listen, I saw your name listed as a consultant on that *Law & Order* episode a while back, and it occurred to me that I might also have a little job for you. Dirty work, as it were. You know what I mean? Right up your alley, I would guess."

St. James is silent for a few seconds. "It just so happens that I'm in the middle of fund-raising for my new group, DANISH— Defenders Against Neo-Islamic Society Haters. If you're talkin' dirty work, I'd need a hundred thousand dollars. Cash. Plus incidentals."

"Not a problem. You'll be doing me a great favor. One I will never forget."

"You had a pretty short memory when we all landed in jail."

"We do what we have to do to survive. I think you know that better than anybody."

"This thing that you want me to do is one of those things that you have to do to survive?" he asks, pushing your buttons.

"For both of us to survive," you reply, pushing his.

15 ↑1.75 ADLAC 22 ↓2.60 ENE 50.50 ↑1.50 TYC 60.25 ↓1.75 MSO 65 ↑2.

Do you actually give a hundred thousand dollars to a hit man to kill Weiss? Go to page 146.

Or do you come to your senses and call it off right now? Go to page 96.

As you turn to step back up onto the sidewalk and out of harm's way, you're suddenly shoved backward by a huge police officer trying to get past you to save the woman. The impact sends you flying into her, knocking her out of the way of the approaching cab. You, on the other hand, fall down right in its path. It runs over your left leg, snapping your femur in half.

You're immediately surrounded by a crowd of people and can hear someone screaming for an ambulance.

A rotund middle-aged man wearing earmuffs looks down at you and then up at the billboard.

"Hey, that's that guy! Harry! Look, he's on that poster!"

Everyone looks up at the poster and then back down at you. Several men lift you up and onto the sidewalk. "He's a hero!" says one of them. As you start to pass out from shock, you notice the policeman who shoved you staring at you and nodding his head while frowning.

Several hours later, surrounded by family and flowers, you're watching CNN, where the headline is: WHITE COLLAR HERO. You're on every newscast, and a clip of the Hispanic woman saying you saved her life is played over and over again.

Your doctor comes by on his rounds and says that you were lucky it was a clean break and that you should only need the wheelchair for six weeks. "That's the price of heroism," he says, smiling, before going out to be interviewed about his role in your recovery by *X-Ray: The Magazine for the Young, Single Doctor.*

Your wife is beaming with pride, and Apple is chattering away into her cell phone, telling all her friends that her dad, "like, almost died."

5 ↑1.75 ADLAC 22 ↓2.60 ENE 50.50 ↑1.50 TYC 60.25 ↓1.75 MSO 65 ↑2.50

Go to page 70.

When you balk at Laufetter's suggestion, you expect a double whammy of trouble. First, you'll have to deal with her. And second, she's likely to trash you in the profile, perhaps even violating journalistic ethics and printing what you told her about Kove. She did just sleep with an interview subject, after all—hardly the most appropriate behavior.

From a personal perspective, she seems to take your decision gracefully, but you're worried about what she might write in a fit of pique. It comes as a complete shock, then, when the profile of you in the *Ivy Business Review* is another of her legendary blowjobs, without a hint of how you got the no-bid contract for the T-shirts. She sends you a copy of the issue with a note that says, "Thanks for a great interview. You come out a winner in it, even though you were a loser with me. Good luck, SL."

Tough as nails, you think. *Maybe I dodged a bullet there.*

Meanwhile your scientists come through with the T-shirts and even manage to outsource production to a company in Bangalore, India. Fleece takes a short-lived beating in the press for being yet another company to export American jobs overseas. But once you manage to communicate that the company has no intention of laying off a single person, and is merely hiring *more* people to meet with the increased demand, the stories take a positive turn. You are lauded as a dexterous CEO who operates successfully in both the fashion and military realms.

You begin delivering the shirts on schedule, and you hear through Carlucci that Kove—and by extension, the president—is quite happy with the quick turnaround. Fleece is even included in a *New York Times Magazine* story on futuristic military equipment. You pose for the two-page spread wearing the military gear and camouflage face paint to bring out your blue eyes.

You are so busy with the combination of meetings, interviews, and society events that you instruct Carson Rodriguez to build a discreet bathroom in the corner of your office so that you don't have to take the time to walk down the hall when nature calls during the day. He protests at first, saying it will destroy the "balance" he's worked so hard to achieve, but he finally succumbs to your aesthetic vision when you threaten to fire him.

Go to page 59.

You spin around a little too quickly to face your would-be captor. "Yuu'rrre a cop! I haven't done anythhiiiing wrong. Being drunk isn't a crime last time I checked," you say, trying to sound as sober as humanly possible.

The man stares back at you without saying a word. But he doesn't move an inch.

You look down at his jacket and notice the bulge again. The wire! If you can get that away from him, there will be nothing to incriminate you. You lunge toward him, getting ahold of both lapels, and tear his jacket open, sending the buttons flying off in several directions. At this point he starts fighting back and sends you reeling backward onto the sidewalk. Just before he jumps on top of you, you notice what was making the bulge in his jacket. An iPod.

The sound of the commotion brings people rushing out of the bar, and before you know it, several men are holding you down.

"Isn't that the guy who makes bulletproof clothing?" someone says. "Rich bastard."

"I don't know who it is," says Wingtips, "but somebody call the cops. He attacked me without any provocation, and I want to press charges." He turns toward you. "I'm going to sue your ass, fucko."

Minutes later the cops show up, and you're hoisted up off the ground, handcuffed, and deposited in the back of a police car, where you promptly pass out completely.

15 ↑1.75 ADLAC 22 ↓2.60 ENE 50.50 ↑1.50 TYC 60.25 ↓1.75 MSO 65 ↑2.

Go to page 69.

Things have never gone so well for Fleece. America is caught up in patriotic fervor, and it's almost treasonous *not* to buy Silk Armor. Everything is selling like hotcakes, and the army asks for a second batch of T-shirts six months ahead of schedule.

By winter the company's profile has risen to such a degree that you actually warm to your wife's long-standing desire to cochair the "Let Them Eat Cake" Charity, which raises money to supply public schools with desserts. You arrive at the event in a carriage straight out of Cinderella. The program describes you as the "King and Queen" of the year's most-watched charity event.

You have reached a level of success that all CEOs dream about. Not only do you have the money, but now you've also got the fame. You're a celebrity in your own right. Tiger Woods is asking you to play golf with him, you get personal invitations from politicians to join them for lunch, and everybody wants you to come to this gallery opening or that restaurant debut.

And it all starts to go to your head.

You start to forget people's names. You stop taking advice from Araz and Jeff, instead dictating to them not just which ads the company will run, but also the exact wording in each. You make visitors to your office wait at least forty-five minutes before you greet them—and then you cut them off midmeeting by telling them you've got something else on your schedule, and you wish the meeting hadn't started so late.

Worst of all, you start treating Fawn like a plain old secretary. You comment on her natty clothes and tell her to get a new wardrobe or not bother coming in to work. To add insult to injury, you hire a new, younger girl to work alongside Fawn. She threatens to quit, but a pay raise and title bump to "executive liaison" placate her bruised ego.

Go to page 13.

"I'm not accusing you of anything, Jennifer. I'm just trying to get to the bottom of this mystery. It was you who projected huge sales of this product. It was you who had us order double the inventory. It is you who will stand to make more money in commissions this year than I make running this place. So I'm having a hard time believing that anyone other than you is the source of these bogus sales." You're beginning to shake from trying to contain your anger.

"Again, I have no idea what you're talking about. I've never been in a warehouse in my life. But if we really do have an inventory surplus on our hands, there's only one way to make it through this quarter relatively unscathed. We can use massive discounts to convince retailers to purchase next season's product right now. We don't have to ship it to them, they don't even have to pay us right now, we just have to book the sales so that they show up in this quarter's numbers."

You lean back in your chair, exasperated by what you are hearing. "Jennifer, that's called channel stuffing. We can go to jail for that."

"Sure, we could. But we won't. Why? Because how is anyone going to find out? Our customers will be happy because of the lower prices. Our investors will be happy because we hit our projections. And everyone will be ecstatic at how successful our company has become! It's a no-brainer." Jennifer punctuates her sentence by popping one last Thin Mint into her mouth.

Do you take the advice of someone who is obviously untrustworthy but has the killer instinct it takes to survive in this business? Go to page 8.

Or do you fire Estrangelo on the spot and tell her to "fuck off" while she's cleaning out her desk? Go to page 138.

"Consider it a deal," you say, wondering whether you've just made the smartest—or the dumbest—business decision of your career.

"Great," he replies. "I'll have someone send up the specs this afternoon. Of course, I'll need to create the appearance of an open bidding process. Just submit the appropriate paperwork when we send it up to you, and we'll award Fleece the business regardless of any competing bids." He hangs up.

Already you're having second thoughts. A no-bid contract, while obviously evidence of favoritism, didn't strike you as crossing some sort of moral or legal boundary. But a rigged bidding process? That sounds more like the insurance industry than the fashion world. Don't they record calls people make from the Pentagon? You picture yourself sitting in the dock during a corruption trial, the jury shell-shocked as they listen to you say, "Consider it a deal."

You chuckle at your own paranoia and reach for your phone. Fleece is now a government contractor. If you're lucky, the T-shirts will become a cultural phenomenon as well—like camouflage pants—and urban and suburban teenagers who've never even held a gun will soon be buying them.

Your first call is to Araz and Jeff. You give them the good news and tell them to start mocking up a few ideas for marketing the T-shirts. They're ecstatic.

You then call your wife. She's not so enthused. "Honey, we're *against* the war in Iraq," she says. "And you hate the president. Why do you want to help him?"

"What are you talking about?" you reply. "We're helping the soldiers. Protecting them so that they can get back home safely. And this contract is going to propel us into the upper echelon of clothing companies. It's good business; it's not like I'm contributing to the president's re-election campaign."

"I just hope you know what you're doing," she says, sounding overly melodramatic. After all, you're talking about a contract to make T-shirts.

"Trust me, honey. I do."

The next month is a whirlwind of activity. Sippowicz was true to his word—the contract was rammed through with nary a peep—and the office is a bees' nest of activity, with designers and scientists sitting hunched together trying to meet the aggressive deadline demanded by the Pentagon.

Once you are confident in the likelihood of success, you issue a press release with the good news. Investors react giddily, buying Fleece stock in droves. You even get a phone call from the editor of the *Ivy Business Review,* asking if you'd like to be the subject of a story in the magazine. You readily accept, knowing full well her penchant for profiles that seem more like blowjobs than legitimate business analyses. You agree to head upstate in a few weeks for a couple of days of interviews.

And you can't stop spouting military metaphors. "This office is running like a well-oiled military machine," you say one day to Fawn as she stares back at you with amusement. You also decide that it's time to redecorate your office. With this contract, the company is looking like it will triple sales this year, so who would begrudge you—the steward of its success—an upgrade of Fleece's very own "central command"? Plus you've got to get those bookshelves put back at a normal height, as it's killing your back every time you have to lean down just to grab a magazine.

You ask Fawn whom she thinks the best person to rethink your workspace would be. She looks at you the way Apple does when you try to pretend you're interested in her new favorite bands.

"Carson Rodriguez, obviously," she replies. "He's the guy from *Fabulous Eye for the Corporate Guy.* He did Harry Kravitz's office on Central Park South and created this effect like a vanishing pool. When you look toward the park, it feels like you're actually *in* the park."

"Well, go ahead and call him then," you say. "The *Ivy Business Review* will be sending a photographer down here to take some pictures of me sometime soon, and I want the office to make me look like the successful CEO that I really am."

Go to page 105.

You feel a rush of adrenaline as the words come out of your mouth: "It's a deal, Wolfe. I'll buy the team. Have your people draw up the contract."

You call your private banker at TownGroup and tell him that you are going to draw down $600 million from Fleece's line of credit. He is a little nervous at first, but he's swayed by the calculation of the interest on a $600 million loan. You've got your money, and now you're going to go out and get your team.

E 15 ↑1.75 ADLAC 22 ↓2.60 ENE 50.50 ↑1.50 TYC 60.25 ↓1.75 MSO 65 ↑2.

Go to page 177.

You decide to call Page Six first. The voice mail picks up after just one ring. "Ian St. Patrick here. Page Six. If you have dirt, please press one. If you have *dirty* dirt, please press two. If you're calling to complain about an item in the paper, please get over yourself." You press one and wait for the beep.

"Hello, I'm returning a call you placed to Fleece Industries earlier today. I'm the CEO. I'm not sure what you need from me, but . . ."

Your second line is ringing. You decide to leave it at that and hang up on St. Patrick's voice mail. You hit line two and say, "Hello."

"This is Ian St. Patrick at Page Six," says the voice on the other end of the line. "Sorry about that. I was talking to one of the Baldwin brothers. But I'm glad we have a chance to talk. We hear you were at Tyree Stubbs's house the night he groped a woman a few months ago. Care to comment?"

"Uh, not really," you say. "I did drop by his house that night, but I don't know anything about . . ."

"Thanks! That's all we need." St. Patrick hangs up.

You call Fawn and tell her to have accounts payable cancel any uncashed checks issued to Stubbs. Then you pick up the phone and dial the number that the police left for you.

Go to page 77.

You stop to take a deep breath, knowing how angry Barry will be when he finds out that you did this behind his back.

"Hmm . . . telling one of your clients that another one is selling. Now that would be insider trading, wouldn't it, Felix? Jesus, man, don't you read the papers?"

"Oh, right," he says. "Okay, forget it. I've got to go, though. If you want these shares sold today, I need to get right on it."

You hang up thinking that at least you'll come out of all of this with $70 million or so. Not a bad day's work. Barry, of course, will probably not think to sell—he's a lawyer, after all—and he'll be left with precious little for all his years of service. *Oh well*, you think. *That sucks for him.*

You call Barry back to finish the conversation. When he comes into your office, he's even more ashen than before.

"Seven more deaths. A recon unit was ambushed by a bunch of insurgents with pellet guns—*pellet* guns—and the fucking shirts couldn't even stop those. We're going to be sued by all these families if the government itself doesn't shut us down. . . . What happened? I tested the shirts out myself, with you, back when we first started selling them. They withstood machine guns. And now a pellet gun rips through one and kills a kid?"

You sit back and think. What the hell could have happened? What changed . . . ?

Bangalore. *Bangalore!* Once you got the army contract, you outsourced production to India. You gave them the specs but never actually saw any evidence that they tested their own version of the T-shirts. Some asshole who's probably paying his staff ten cents an hour is cutting corners on you.

"Barry, who is our partner in India?"

"Some guy named Om Daddy. Never met him, but he lived in the United States for years before going back over there to start an outsourcing conglomerate."

"Well, Barry, maybe we're not as fucked as we think. Most people in this country are already grumbling about Indians stealing their jobs. How do you think they're going to react when we tell them that Indians are at fault for their kids dying? Let's get a press release ready to issue, as though we were caught off guard by the one coming from the government tomorrow. It will be a perfect deflection on our part."

"You're a genius," says Barry.

5 ↑ 1.75 ADLAC 22 ↓ 2.60 ENE 50.50 ↑ 1.50 TYC 60.25 ↓ 1.75 MSO 65 ↑ 2.50

Go to page 76.

Weiss walks right up to your desk and leans into your face. "You think you can fire me? Are you for real? I know everything. I know where all the skeletons are hidden. I'll call the *Wall Street Journal* right now. I don't give a shit. This is how you repay me for all that I've done for you?"

Weiss is more agitated than you've ever seen him and can barely contain himself.

Over his left shoulder you notice the Remington on your wall. You think back to your discussion with Moneyhouse. Was he actually suggesting murder? It seems impossible. But with Weiss threatening to bring Fleece down with him, all of a sudden it doesn't seem so implausible an idea. You, of course, can't do it yourself, but do you really need to *get rid of* Weiss?

"Weiss, Weiss, please. I'm doing nothing of the sort. I'm not going to fire you. But you clearly couldn't handle all the work you've had these last several months. You got us into this situation. And Ms. Sutinis is just an experienced accountant who will help get us out. Calm down."

Weiss visibly calms down.

"Now, come on. Go back to your office, and the three of us will have a meeting this afternoon and split up responsibilities going forward."

Thankfully, Weiss leaves. So now what are you going to do?

15 ↑1.75 ADLAC 22 ↓2.60 ENE 50.50 ↑1.50 TYC 60.25 ↓1.75 MSO 65 ↑2.

Do you actually consider having Weiss murdered? Go to page 186.
Or do you do the sensible thing and find a way to silence him without actually having the poor man killed? Go to page 232.

You wake up in the morning with a searing pain below your left eye, which seems to be swollen shut. You manage to open your right eye and see a gray concrete ceiling above you.

"Honey, what's going on . . . ," you say, reaching for your wife. Only then do you realize that you're in a cell.

There's a guard sitting outside it. "You're in jail, sweetheart," he says.

You sit up and reach up to your left eye. It all starts painfully coming back to you now. All those scotches. Wingtips punched you in the face. The cops showed up.

"I had a rough day, officer," you say, trying to put on your best face. "I was pretty drunk. I don't usually get that way. I didn't hurt that guy at all, did I?"

The cop looks back at you as if you're crazy.

"Which guy?" he says. "The guy from the bar? Or the guy you had killed yesterday? You told us all about it. They actually even found the body late last night. It was underneath a dock in Red Hook. He'd been strangled. And he had an American flag stuffed down his throat. You're one twisted motherfucker."

"I think I'm going to need to call my lawyer," you say.

The end

On your first day back at work, the Fleece elevator doors open and you are wheeled out into the lobby of your office by your male nurse, Phrixus. A strapping, muscular Greek, he had gained momentary celebrity of his own when, as a dead lifter in the 2004 Athens games, he was thrown out for life for steroid use. You don't care if Phrixus uses steroids, as long as he can get you in and out of your chair with the least amount of pain possible.

You are greeted with a standing ovation, your second such greeting this year. When you enter your own office, you notice that all of your shelves, your credenza, and your desk have been lowered to fit your new sedentary position—compliments of Araz and Jeff, who have little work to do marketing the Harry brand, since your much-publicized act of bravery sent sales through the roof.

You start to find that people who were once disagreeable to work with are now very congenial in their dealings with you. Logistical problems and delays with suppliers and manufacturers that had heretofore been plaguing you start magically disappearing. And Fawn has shown you the more positive aspects of making love in a wheelchair, which is all the more easy with the tear-away business suits you had your designers come up with because you were having difficulty getting in and out of your clothes. They come with Velcro strips down each side so that you can get in and out of them in just a few seconds. (Araz suggested hiring a streaker to endorse the suits at the Super Bowl, but you told him he'd better not even think of trying to market them that way.)

The mayor gives you the key to the city, which also doubles as a key to the gates of Gramercy Park, a fact you discover over a porterhouse dinner with him in Gracie Mansion. You're invited back to ring the opening bell at the New York Stock Exchange, an unprecedented event in the exchange's history. Ricky Dey even presents you with a bronze buttonwood tree, a gift usually reserved for foreign dignitaries and pint-size pop stars.

Meanwhile business is on fire. The virtuous cycle of interest in Fleece clothing and Fleece stock has business reporters falling all over themselves to write fawning profiles of you and your company. Huge orders from retailers around the country have the combined effect of allowing you to raise prices while also negotiating more favorable deals with suppliers.

You find yourself actually looking forward to the Fleece board meeting—yet another first—all thanks to that earnest policeman in Times Square.

15 ↑ 1.75 ADLAC 22 ↓ 2.60 ENE 50.50 ↑ 1.50 TYC 60.25 ↓ 1.75 MSO 65 ↑ 2.50

Go to page 92.

You're sitting on the plane heading back to New York, still chuckling at the image of Kovacs running out of his office after you threw the stone in a perfect arc through his window. He ran out, screaming that a sniper had tried to shoot him, without noticing you standing behind a telephone pole laughing hysterically. Who knows, maybe the guy will use the event to get himself in the paper and somehow turn the "attack on his life" into an opportunity to blow another $100 million on another ridiculous buddy movie.

Thanks to a Valium and a couple of Bloody Marys in the President's lounge at LAX, you sleep from the moment you sit down in first class, and awake only when the wheels touch down at La Guardia.

You'd expected a bit of a contentious conversation with your wife, given the lack of communication during your trip, but she is actually happy to have you home and won't stop talking about the new tufted ottoman she bought for a mere $6,500 from Thomasville.

"That's the thing you put your feet on, right?" you ask.

"Not on this one. Nobody is putting their feet on this one," she says.

You roll your eyes and tell her that you're still a little groggy from the flight and that you're going to turn in early. You go into your den and call Tiffany on your cell phone.

"Hello, sexy," she answers.

"Hi. I just wanted to tell you I had a fantasy about you and me doing it on the plane," you whisper into the phone.

"What? I can't hear you."

"I'm whispering because I'm home."

"You'll have to speak up."

"I had a fantasy about you and me doing it on the plane!" you say, almost yelling but catching yourself.

"Doing what on a plane? I'm sorry, but I'm in a restaurant. It's too loud here."

Exasperated, you hang up the phone. You'll call her tomorrow. You leave your den and go upstairs to your room. You fall asleep thinking about Tiffany.

15 ↑ 1.75 ADLAC 22 ↓ 2.60 ENE 50.50 ↑ 1.50 TYC 60.25 ↓ 1.75 MSO 65 ↑ 2.5

Go to page 141.

"You know," you yell to Araz, "maybe we should start trying to outfit entire teams with Fleece sportswear. There's that company that only makes baseball uniforms and they're really successful."

"What was that last part?" yells Araz. "Who's successful?"

You're sitting on the toilet in your private bathroom, holding a meeting through the door. You'd heard somewhere that Lyndon Johnson used to hold meetings in the Oval Office while on the throne, and you figured that if he could do it, why can't you?

You stand up, flush the toilet, and emerge from the cedar-paneled room. "I said there's a company that's been quite successful making uniforms. We need to build Fleece's athletic portfolio. Think of it: We already have Stubbs wearing our gear off the court. It's only a short leap to getting a whole team to wear our clothing while they're actually playing! Wearing Silk Armor while on national TV! They could then switch into bulletproof suits when they go out to rap with their homeys after the game."

"Homeys?" says Jeff. "Since when do you use the word 'homeys'?"

"Since you better watch out or I'll fire you, that's when," you reply, quite seriously. You notice that your fly is undone and zip it up unabashedly in front of everyone assembled. Nothing embarrasses you anymore. You're like a supermodel who can strip naked backstage at a fashion show in the middle of a few hundred people—you know that people are staring more in awe of you than anything else.

"What about the New Jersey Corporals?" you ask the table, which includes Jeff, Araz, and three cute Harvard MBAs you hired after they'd arrived at the office for their interviews wearing matching outfits. You've had numerous fantasies about them since, and invite them into any meeting conceivable. "The American Football League team."

"What about them?" asks Jeff.

"Who owns them again? Desmond Wolfe? Someone get him on the horn. I'll offer to make his team's uniforms for free, and we'll take it from there. Okay, then, this meeting is finished. Everybody out."

5 ↑ 1.75 ADLAC 22 ↓ 2.60 ENE 50.50 ↑ 1.50 TYC 60.25 ↓ 1.75 MSO 65 ↑ 2.50

Go to page 82.

You spend the next twenty-four hours preparing Fleece's response to the inevitable announcement by the army, stopping only to take a call from Felix, who says he has successfully sold your shares.

You start by having your scientists take Fleece's original T-shirts and test them alongside those made by Om Daddy's Indian outfit. Your instincts were right. Only the Indian T-shirts were defective. You then have the components analyzed and discover that Om hadn't used a single ounce of the polymer shield in the mix for the material.

The government makes its announcement around 2:00 P.M. Fleece stock, of course, starts a steep descent immediately, but you wait to give the appearance of finding out the news at the same time as everyone else. You refuse all phone calls from reporters and sit with Barry drinking scotch in your office, pretending that you're trying to find a way out of the mess.

After the market closes, you issue your own press release saying that while the company is genuinely sorry for the deaths of the soldiers, an internal investigation has turned up evidence of fraud by your Indian partners. You add that Om Daddy has operations in the United States, hoping that any grieving parent looking to sue someone for their children's deaths will go after him and not you. While it is a Friday afternoon and the markets are officially closed, aftermarket orders of Fleece show strong interest in buying the stock.

The plan works like a charm. The Saturday papers paint a picture of you as a CEO who has the best interests of American youth in mind, but who has been deceived by unscrupulous foreigners. Some, of course, go even further, suggesting that terrorists had infiltrated Om Daddy's factory in Bangalore and sabotaged the production process. The most extreme try to tie the failure of the shirts to a diabolical plan hatched by the president to get re-elected.

E 15 ↑1.75 ADLAC 22 ↓2.60 ENE 50.50 ↑1.50 TYC 60.25 ↓1.75 MSO 65 ↑2.

Go to page 116.

The call to the police is a snap. They ask if you'd been at Stubbs's house the night of the incident, and you tell them the same thing you told Page Six. The officer is quite polite—he even tells you that his wife is a big fan of your show—and says he doesn't think the police will need anything else from you.

Stubbs is ultimately vindicated. It turns out that he'd been playing blackjack on the cruise on the night in question, and a dealer in the ship's casino testified that Stubbs had been at the table all night, losing hundreds of thousands of dollars. You manage to get another check out to California with some excuse before he realizes that you'd been prepared to abandon him.

Your Page Six mention has a totally unexpected result. It says only that you had been at the party and nothing more. That only adds fuel to the fire of your fame—Kovacs even puts together a couple of ads saying "*The Simple Stitch* Makes Page Six." Your fame among women, particularly middle-aged women, only increases.

Your wife's reaction is a different matter. You have to admit to her that the reason you hadn't called her back from LA that night was not because you'd fallen asleep exhausted, but because you'd been at Tyree's house. You come clean about your partying in LA—the booze, the drugs, and your "flirting" with girls. You join Alcoholics Anonymous, which becomes not so anonymous when you and your wife talk about your new sober life on *Oprah*. Tiffany is so grateful about the introduction to Kovacs—he cast her in a remake of *Gigli*—that she keeps quiet about your affair.

You remain on *People*'s Sexiest Man Alive list for four straight years. You and your wife become the icon of the ideal married couple, gracing the covers of *Redbook* and *Better Homes and Gardens*. You even get a chance to meet Johnny Depp at a party at the Time Warner Center and make an unprecedented endorsement deal with the expat star. He's been wearing Harry ever since.

The end

The rest of the meeting is as painful as a root canal. As everyone files out you see that not a single Fleece hat has been taken. You start to shove them back into the bag when Moneyhouse walks back in and puts his arm around you like a Little League coach.

"It's all right, pal. You can't win these people over with hats and handshakes. A nice chunk of Fleece stock will win their hearts, though. They're businessmen. We are in the business of making money. You are in the business of making clothes. Stick to that. We'll take care of the rest."

You can't even think of how to respond, so you just nod.

"About the Nigeria deal," he says. "Just thought I'd let you know that everything worked out perfectly. A couple of my own employees invested in the venture, it's off and running, and we've moved the liability off your books. Fleece is clean as a whistle. Except, of course, for one thing. Too many people know about this."

"Barry?" you say to Moneyhouse. "Barry wouldn't tell a soul. He's my oldest friend. And he's got a lot tied up in this as well."

"I'm not talking about Barry," he says. "I'm talking about Weiss. He's a liability to all of us. You'll get rid of him, right?"

Moneyhouse then looks up at the wall at portraits of himself and his former partner, Stonecutter. You flash back to the *New York Post* headline from several years before: SOGGY SANTA. It was a story that described how Stonecutter had washed up on the shores of Staten Island in a waterlogged Santa suit.

Is he talking about murder? He can't be. The police never connected Moneyhouse to Stonecutter's death, and it was ultimately ruled an accident. (Ironically, Stonecutter won a Darwin Award that year for the dumbest way to die. With a blood alcohol level four times the legal limit, he'd reportedly tried to swim across the Hudson to his home in Hoboken in the middle of winter.)

You look at Moneyhouse. He seems to be growing impatient.

"Of course," you say back to him. "I'll get rid of him."

15 ↑1.75 ADLAC 22 ↓2.60 ENE 50.50 ↑1.50 TYC 60.25 ↓1.75 MSO 65 ↑2.

Go to page 192.

The taxi pulls up in front of your building. You take the elevator up to the executive floor, storm by Fawn, and kick open the door of your office. Weiss is huddled in the corner, crying softly.

He stands up as you come in and says through tears, "Let me explain, boss. I can explain everything. Really." When he sees the look on your face, he sits back down. You tell the security guards they can leave the office.

"You piece of shit, Weiss. What the hell could you have been thinking? The company was doing fine. Why did you have to cook the books? For what? We were going public anyway. You were going to be a rich man. Now we could all go to jail."

Weiss chokes out a garbled response. "I'm sorry, boss. It was just that with the second kid and all, and my mortgage and all the money I lost in the tech bubble, I really needed to make that bonus last year, and . . ."

There's a knock at the door and Fawn pokes her head in. "Um, I didn't want to interrupt," she says, "but there's a man here who says he's from the Securities and Exchange Commission."

All the color leaves Weiss's face. "The feds," he whispers. *What an asshole*, you think.

"Fawn, make him comfortable in the conference room. I'll be there shortly."

You turn to Weiss. "We're not finished here. I can't believe you. I hired you because you were in trouble and this is how you pay me back—" You cut yourself off. This is not the time to get riled up. You have to cool down so that everything will appear hunky-dory to the SEC.

"Don't puke on my couch," you say as you turn toward the door. "And don't even think of leaving this office, unless it's by the window."

15 ↑ 1.75 ADLAC 22 ↓ 2.60 ENE 50.50 ↑ 1.50 TYC 60.25 ↓ 1.75 MSO 65 ↑ 2.50

Go to page 88.

The next half hour is most certainly one during which you wouldn't have wanted any interruptions. Scott, who has long coveted his boss's job, explains to you a systematic program of fraud that he stumbled across when trying to reconcile sales and returns data. And he's pretty sure Estrangelo is behind all of it.

"She told you to order fifty million dollars' worth of stretch workout gear last week, right?"

"Yeah, for the weekend cross-trainer. I can't believe how successful it's been. It's a gold mine. Why?" You have no idea where he's going with this.

"Well," he says. "The Newark warehouse called me last week asking why one of our trucks was bringing back a complete shipment of the stretch workout gear as returns, when it didn't look like they'd even gone anywhere."

"What are you saying, Donny? We get returns all the time."

"It looks like Estrangelo was putting in huge orders, entering them into the sales database, and having the trucks drive from one state to another and then logging them as returns. Because our front- and back-end systems don't yet speak to each other, it was taking weeks, if not months, for the reconciliation to occur. She's been goosing sales to meet her projections. Not only have we not sold much stretch workout gear at all, but you also just put another fifty million dollars into the system. We're going to miss next quarter's sales projections by a country mile. And our credit line is pretty much tapped. We're headed for a cash crunch."

You're screwed. Missing your first quarter of financial projections as a public company will destroy Fleece stock. Running out of money could even destroy the company itself. Wall Street lore is full of stories of companies that went public only to be demolished by unhappy analysts and short sellers within months. You're about to become the latest sad tale of a company that couldn't run with the big dogs.

Unless, that is, you can somehow manage to get things back

on track and make sure that your shareholders don't catch wind of Estrangelo's misdeeds.

You regain a little of your composure. "Thanks, Donny," you say. "You know, if what you say is true, Estrangelo will be out on the street before the day is over. And her job will be yours for the taking. But I really should get her side of the story before I make any decisions."

Donny nods, suppressing a smile, and heads out the door.

"Fawn! Get Estrangelo in here. Immediately!"

15 ↑ 1.75 ADLAC 22 ↓ 2.60 ENE 50.50 ↑ 1.50 TYC 60.25 ↓ 1.75 MSO 65 ↑ 2.50

Go to page 23.

Just over a week later you're sitting in the Four Seasons eating oysters with Desmond Wolfe. The usual media and corporate titans are all there having lunch, and it's a little more crowded than usual because Veronica's Mystery lingerie models are staying at the hotel for the week and all the Viagra poppers want to catch a glimpse of their heavenly bodies. Except Wolfe, that is.

You didn't think he'd want to eat out so publicly after yesterday's breaking news, but his office had called and insisted that he still wanted to keep all of his appointments. (You nearly cancelled the meeting yourself—it had occurred to you that being seen in public with Wolfe might taint your growing reputation—but Jeff and Araz reminded you of the number-one maxim of fame: No publicity is bad publicity. "We're also an open-minded company," you said to the two of them, marveling at your own capacity for empty corporate platitudes.)

Twenty-four hours before this lunch, Wolfe shook both New Jersey and the sports world to their roots. It turned out he'd been having an illicit homosexual affair with the head of security at the stadium, and the man, who had had no previous experience in security at all, had tried to extort money out of Wolfe in exchange for keeping quiet.

Wolfe, though, would have none of it. A proud man who'd been born in Costa Rica and was adopted and raised by a couple from Cincinnati, he took to the airwaves and delivered a history-making speech in which he declared, "I am a gay Central American," effectively heading off his blackmailer's threat to expose him.

Yet here he is, just one day later, in the most public of high-power noshing spots. He seems relieved more than anything else. Before you even have a chance to dab the oyster juice sliding down your chin, Wolfe launches into a proposal you never would have anticipated.

15 ↑1.75 ADLAC 22 ↓2.60 ENE 50.50 ↑1.50 TYC 60.25 ↓1.75 MSO 65 ↑2.5

Go to page 213.

You find out what Kove meant the very next day when you're back in New York. Fawn pokes her head in your office and says there's a man who claims he's from the Pentagon on the phone.

"I thought he was joking, but he seems quite serious," she says.

You pick up the line.

"Hello?"

"Is this the CEO of Fleece Industries?" says a voice.

"Yes, it is. Who's calling?"

"My name is Wolf Sippowicz," he says. "I'm calling on instructions from Ralph Kove. As a favor to Fred Carlucci, we'd like to offer you the opportunity to enter into a no-bid contract to outfit our men in Iraq with bulletproof T-shirts. I didn't even know there was such a thing, but he says you're for real. Do you make bulletproof clothing? We don't want any fleece—it's way too hot over there—just plain white T-shirts."

You nearly drop the phone. "Ah, yes, we do make bulletproof clothing. We could easily make T-shirts if you needed them. How many would you be thinking about?"

"Well," he says. "We have one hundred and fifty thousand servicemen on the ground, and if you add in potential reservists, that will get us to about two hundred thousand. Seven shirts apiece makes one-point-four million. If they work, we could be talking about several million more."

"Of course they work," you say, somewhat insulted by the insinuation, but at the same time calculating what kind of profits you could make from such a contract. You briefly think back to the early days of Fleece, when you were testing the clothing by firing handguns at fully dressed mannequins and dousing scarves and pantyhose in gasoline and trying to light them on fire.

"Well then," he says, "consider it a firm order. We'll need the million-four as soon as you can get them to us."

A no-bid contract? From the government? This would change everything. If toilet seats sell for a thousand dollars apiece, you can't even imagine what they'd pay for the shirts.

15 ↑ 1.75 ADLAC 22 ↓ 2.60 ENE 50.50 ↑ 1.50 TYC 60.25 ↓ 1.75 MSO 65 ↑ 2.

Do you tell him you'll start making the shirts tomorrow? Go to page 61.
Or do you ask for time to think it over? Go to page 43.

During the five-hour flight back to New York, you mull over the concept of shifting Fleece's branding campaign to revolve entirely around you; the idea starts to seem better with each passing moment.

You can launch a new "signature" line of Fleece clothing, using your college nickname—Harry. (Well, it was actually "Hairy" because of an unfortunate back hair problem that your wife insisted you take care of with electrolysis as soon as you started making real money. But you've since convinced yourself that your college buddies were really calling you "Harry.") You scratch out a few slogans on a cocktail napkin:

Fleece, by Harry
Harry's Choice
Everybody Loves Harry
Harry Omnimedia

And the new clothing lines:

Baby Harry
Harry Republic
Harry Exchange
Harry's Secret
Harry One
Old Harry
Club Harry

By the time the plane is passing over Pennsylvania, you've made up your mind. You're going to be the centerpiece of a radical new marketing campaign the likes of which the clothing industry has never seen before. And it's going to work.

Why? Because you're the perfect front man for Fleece's rugged but comfortable image. Everyone who meets you thinks you're charming. You're a family man (as far as the public is concerned). You're fit, you're good looking, you have a full head of hair, and you're well spoken. Women obviously love you. Take Tiffany. She's a twenty-two-year-old who could have any man in Hollywood, and she chose you. If you can manage to attach your own personal appeal to Fleece products, they'll practically sell themselves.

You spend the rest of the flight in a giddy state, imagining yourself on a billboard on the West Side Highway in Manhattan. You call your wife from the car on the way back from the airport and tell her that you're sorry, but you won't be home right away, even though you haven't seen her in almost a week. You call Fawn and ask her to tell Jeff McDougal and Araz Matali, your marketing gurus, to meet you in your office in an hour. You've got a lot of work to do.

E 15 ↑1.75 ADLAC 22 ↓2.60 ENE 50.50 ↑1.50 TYC 60.25 ↓1.75 MSO 65 ↑2.

Go to page 10.

You throw the MTV bag on the ground and dive toward the woman. Your aim was dead-on: You smash into her, knocking her backward and out of danger's way. Just then you feel yourself getting pushed, except it's not by another person—it's the taxi. The impact launches you into the air, and you come smashing down on the cab's windshield before rolling over the top of the taxi and onto the street behind its squealing back tires. You barely register the sight of a UPS truck before it drives over your chest and legs. The impact crushes your rib cage and severs your spinal cord.

The only thing you're capable of doing is looking straight up into the sky. Among a sea of faces, you notice your own face looking down at you. The billboard. HARRY NEW YEAR AND MANY MORE!

A rotund middle-aged man wearing earmuffs looks down at you and then up at the billboard.

"Hey, that's that guy! Harry! Look, he's on that poster!"

You die with the crowd turned away from you, looking up at the billboard.

The end

You're standing down the hallway from the conference room. You take a deep breath to compose yourself—it's do or die. You walk up to the door and open it. Fawn is handing the man a bottle of water. "Fawn, may we have the room, please?"

Fawn leaves. The man stands up and extends his hand. "Hi! I'm Jerry Flaxworthy, from the regulatory division of the Securities and Exchange Commission. I'm here for a routine post-IPO visit. We're required to pay a call to all new publicly traded companies. If your in-house counsel is around, I suggest you tell them to join us."

"Actually," you stammer, "this is kind of awkward, but we're going through a transitional phase right now. Our counsel has long maintained that he would stay on until the IPO and then he was going to retire. He actually gave notice this morning and we're looking around for the right replacement."

"It's an unfortunate time to lose your counsel," says Flaxworthy, with a look of corporate concern on his face—a combination of sincere compassion and a splash of suspicion. "No matter, though, if you can find one soon. This is the time in a company's life when it's at its most vulnerable—you've now got to play by the rules of the public markets. It's not your company anymore. It's now partly owned by your investors."

"It's quite the trial by fire," you say, chuckling like a naive rookie, hoping to provoke a parental response from the bureaucrat.

Flaxworthy says nothing and just stares back at you.

You try to change the subject. "Wait a second. Let's walk and talk. How about a tour of the office before we roll up our sleeves and get into the nitty-gritty."

Flaxworthy looks at his watch and, to your great relief, agrees.

E 15 ↑1.75 ADLAC 22 ↓2.60 ENE 50.50 ↑1.50 TYC 60.25 ↓1.75 MSO 65 ↑2

Go to page 127.

You are sitting at the defense table. Carson is no longer sitting at the table with you. Carson copped a plea for his testimony. He has been forced to perform community service by redecorating the New York Institute for the Blind.

The testimony is over. Both the prosecution and the defense have rested. The jury marches into the jury box after three days of deliberation. Your fate is sealed. You're about to live the life of a convict, seeing your daughter once every two months when she visits you in a common area surrounded by America's worst offenders of the law.

You watch the jury file in, and they all look like robots with no capability for feeling or compassion. There's the construction worker, the small Indian man, the lazy man with the loose tie, and the morbidly obese Latino with a different NFL jersey for each day. You've watched all of their expressions and body language for six weeks, and they've been nothing but ice cold. You have no doubt that they're about to send you up the river.

But then you notice the frail old woman. You'd nicknamed her "the Librarian," as she reminded you of old Mrs. Hubel from your grade school library. She walks into the courtroom staring at you—as she has done the whole trial—almost as if she knew you took the book *Valley of the Dolls* without signing it out first. She keeps her gaze on you as she takes her seat. When the foreman of the jury stands to read your verdict, you could swear that she gives you a wink.

Is that something in her eye? you think. *No, she definitely winked.*

You lean over to Conran, not knowing why it would be important, and tell him that you think a juror winked at you.

"What?" he whispers.

"The Librarian! She winked at me!"

"Keep it to yourself until we know what the verdict is."

"All rise!" shouts the sleepy bailiff with the strawberry blond comb-over. As you rise both you and Conran notice that the Librarian is still looking at you.

You turn around and catch sight of all of the reporters in the gallery with their thumbs on their BlackBerrys ready to scoop their fellow journalists with the verdict. You turn back around and face the foreman.

"Has the jury come to a verdict?"

E 15 ↑ 1.75 ADLAC 22 ↓ 2.60 ENE 50.50 ↑ 1.50 TYC 60.25 ↓ 1.75 MSO 65 ↑ 2

Go to page 242.

The show ends with a twist—you tell the camera in private that you're going to fire Bernadette, but when the time comes, you switch your call and say your last "You can't cut it!" to Travis instead. Your living room erupts in shrieks as the teenage girls marvel at the fast one you pulled on a nationwide television audience.

"Quiet! Quiet!" says Apple. "The bloopers are starting. I don't want to miss Dad being a jackass!"

Everyone stares at the screen, which begins with a text message: THANKS FOR THE GOOD TIMES. T AND S.

T and S? you think. *What the hell is that?*

Suddenly the camera is following Tiffany down the hall of the Fleece office. *She'll be happy about that, especially since she wasn't in the last episode at all.*

A voiceover begins: "Designers at Fleece Industries are changing the way America gets dressed in the morning. But the real action at this company is not in front of a drafting board or on the runway. . . ."

What's this? you think. *Where is Kovacs going with this?*

". . . It's in the dark hallways of a studio in Queens, and in the CEO's office."

The scene on the television is suddenly one of Tiffany with her hand on your pants in the hallway of the Queens studio. "I'm pretty good with my right hand myself," she says. It cuts to your office. There's what looks like security camera footage of you sitting behind your desk saying "Come to Papa" to a pixilated Tiffany. The last thing you see, before smashing the television on the floor in front of the horrified room, is Tyree Stubbs saying, "Yeah, I introduced them, but I didn't know he was cheating on his wife with her. He said he wanted to help her career. . . ."

T and S: Tiffany and Stu. They played you like an accordion.

The end

Tiffany & Stu

You arrive at your office the morning of the board meeting practically skipping. (Your doctor was right—you did heal in six weeks—and you've even been able to start jogging again, albeit at quite a slow pace.)

"Fawn, what time is the board meeting again?" you ask as she hands you coffee and a bagel.

"One o'clock," she says. "So don't take one of your three-martini lunches!"

You both laugh, all the more because you've *never* taken a three-martini lunch.

The morning passes quickly, and before you know it, you're standing in front of Fleece's board of directors, using a laser pointer to demonstrate just how far Fleece sales and profits have risen.

The assembled group is one of pure corporate insiders. Three longtime business partners; the CEOs of a few companies whom you met out at Shinnecock; two Wall Streeters; and Barry McTeagle, Fleece's in-house counsel.

"And get this, gentlemen. On the advice of Araz and Jeff, our marketing gurus, we even took the daring gamble of cutting our marketing expenses to zero during the quarter, on the assumption that the favorable press from the incident in Times Square would be enough to drive interest in Fleece. And the gamble worked—as a result, our profit margins jumped from ten to fifteen percent during the quarter, putting another seventy million dollars in Fleece's coffers."

"I think this would be a good time to talk about what we're going to put in *your* coffers for the great job you've been doing," says Ken Hart, the CEO of Eden Pacific, a conglomerate that owns airlines, music stores, and even a pizza delivery business. You're surprised he's even here—he's usually off breeding kangaroos and racing his legion of jet skis in the Florida Keys.

This is the moment when you get uncomfortable in board meetings, however. You know that your compensation is already at absurd levels—last year, for example, you took home $1.5 million—but you're also not the kind of person to leave money on the table if it's there for the taking.

Twenty minutes later you adjourn the meeting and rush back to your office to call your wife and give her the good news: The board not only raised your salary, they also just gave you a $10 million stock grant. A whole host of other perks was included in a confidential agreement that would extend into your retirement. Your wife reminds you of her lifelong dream to own a Tuscan villa, and you remind her of what you've always told her: You're not buying an Italian getaway until you own a private jet that will take you there and back. "And I might just go jet shopping this weekend," you say, without any acknowledgment of the absurdity of such a remark.

5 ↑ 1.75 ADLAC 22 ↓ 2.60 ENE 50.50 ↑ 1.50 TYC 60.25 ↓ 1.75 MSO 65 ↑ 2.50

Go to page 98.

You, Jeff, and Araz stand in the middle of your office facing one another as if in a Mexican standoff—nobody moves until the other draws. The tension of the moment is broken when everyone realizes the ridiculousness of partaking in a reality show, and you all start laughing at once. You look down at your now warm Heineken and say, "We've been in this room too long. Let's go home and get some rest. Tomorrow we'll start in the afternoon, with everybody. We'll get input from the whole staff. I think this can work."

Araz and Jeff nod in weary agreement, and everyone leaves the office.

And what seems like two seconds since the moment you turned off your office lights, you're turning them back on at 6:00 the next morning. Within minutes you're at your desk sipping a large cup of hot chai with a pen in your hand and a yellow legal pad on your lap. You lean back in your chair and begin one of your famous to-do lists that started Fleece in the first place.

> Engage large shareholders
> Reinvigorate the sales staff
> Infuse the office with youth
> Cut dead wood
> Recommit to family
> Cut costs
> Defend the brand-always

Throughout the fall you travel the eastern seaboard, putting the spark back into your shareholder relations. You play infinite holes of golf and sit in countless deep leather chairs talking about the trajectory of the stock market. You listen to anxious investors express their worries about the viability of the new brand, and you assure them that you are not anxious, but excited for the challenge of making it work.

In November you play touch football and cook Thanksgiving dinner for your sales staff of twenty-five. Over spiced beer and pumpkin pie, you talk casually about not only the importance of teamwork, but also the hidden pleasures of it.

You create an intern program that swarms the office with cute young women and ambitious young men who are not afraid to blow past a waddling accountant while sprinting down the hall with a bolt of black watch plaid fabric. The office is loud and busy and sometimes hectic. Any older staff members who complain don't do so for long, because they are let go and replaced by people too inexperienced to be jaded.

All the while, Araz and Jeff are locked away, untouched by any distraction or criticism, as they meticulously build the Harry brand. And as that brand grows, textile suppliers are courting you with increasingly attractive terms of sale, and manufacturing companies are offering their services at rock-bottom prices.

Stepping out of the revolving door of Henri Bendel and into the refreshing crisp air of the Advent season, you've also just finished your holiday shopping. As you wrestle with a hatbox getting into your car, it never felt so good to say to the driver, "Take me home."

5 ↑1.75 ADLAC 22 ↓2.60 ENE 50.50 ↑1.50 TYC 60.25 ↓1.75 MSO 65 ↑2.50

Go to page 132.

"St. James, I've made a terrible mistake," you say. "Please forget that I ever called you."

"Forget this call? It was your press release about making us those stupid clothes—they weren't even bulletproof, by the way—that brought the man down on us. You owe me."

You hang up, throw the phone card in a trash can, and walk back to your office. What on earth has come over you? Murder? Weiss? For God's sake, he's been nothing but loyal. He did exercise bad judgment, but he was really only trying to help the company. You decide that maybe you'll take him out to lunch and figure out a way to make him happy. Hell, you'll give him a bonus this afternoon.

When you arrive back at Fawn's desk, you ask her if she's seen Weiss.

"No, I haven't, actually. He seemed pretty distraught when he came out of your office. I'm sorry about telling him he was fired. I'd just assumed you'd told him."

"Don't worry, Fawn. It's okay. I'm not firing him. It was all a big misunderstanding. I'm going to go find him right now."

You head toward Weiss's office. He's not there. You notice, in passing, that Ms. Sutinis isn't in the office next to his, where you assumed Fawn would put her. You head back to your office and ask Fawn if she's seen Sutinis.

"No, I put her in the office next to Weiss. But I haven't seen her since then," she says.

You pull out your cell phone and call Weiss. No answer. Where the hell could he be? You go back into your office and check your e-mails. There's nothing from Weiss. There's one from Apple, though. The subject line says, "I LOVE YOU, DADDY." You're overtaken with emotion and the wonder of being a parent. *Weiss is a parent*, it occurs to you. What on earth have you been thinking? Having him murdered?

All of a sudden the door of your office flies open and a huge crowd of men in trench coats comes rushing in. Weiss is behind them, pointing at you. "That's him," he says.

E 15 ↑1.75 ADLAC 22 ↓2.60 ENE 50.50 ↑1.50 TYC 60.25 ↓1.75 MSO 65 ↑2

Go to page 104.

Carlucci was right. The very next day, officials from the Federal Trade Commission show up at every single Fleece distribution center in the country and slap them with injunctions for failure to maintain complete records. No trucks are allowed to leave any of the premises, and the entire company grinds to a halt.

You leave several messages for Sippowicz, pleading for him to let you take on the Iraq business, but he doesn't return any of your calls.

After two weeks of untangling the company from all the red tape Kove had wrapped it up in, you finally get the trucks on the road again, but you've had two weeks of zero sales. Investors do as expected and give Fleece stock a bit of a haircut. But that isn't the end of it: As the quarter goes on, several of your customers demand discounts for all the business they themselves lost when you were unable to ship them Fleece goods. Your sales team ultimately succeeds in persuading you to relent for fear of losing their business entirely.

The Harry ad campaign turns into a complete travesty, with editors taking potshots every chance they get.

"Harry's no Hare," suggests the *New York Times*, complete with a picture of your face on the body of a tortoise.

"Harried Harry," counters the *Wall Street Journal*, in a story that meticulously deconstructs Fleece's foundering marketing efforts.

By the time the quarter comes to an end, you're relieved it's over. You'll break the bad news to Wall Street and then hopefully start with a clean slate. Every company slips up now and then, you think, and Wall Street has a short memory. Hell, you didn't even slip up per se—you ran into a couple of corrupt and vindictive politicians, including the president, and you paid the price. As far as you can tell, they only wanted to teach you a lesson and will hopefully leave you and your company alone from here on in.

The worst, you think, has already passed.

5 ↑1.75 ADLAC 22 ↓2.60 ENE 50.50 ↑1.50 TYC 60.25 ↓1.75 MSO 65 ↑2.50

Go to page 107.

The windfall, however, leaves you facing a decision you've never faced before. Where are you supposed to put ten million dollars that you might want to get your hands on at a moment's notice? Not in the bank, surely. You want that ten million dollars to be making more money for you than a meager 2 percent savings rate.

And while Felix, your broker at TownGroup, seems entirely capable of the simple task of keeping track of how much stock you own, you certainly don't want him making investment decisions for you. But you also don't want to invest in something you can't sell quickly.

You get your answer in an unlikely venue: at your physical therapist's office. One day while you are changing out of your sweat suit back into street clothes, you notice Dylan Starr, the young, rugged actor whose career had been raked over the coals because of a torrid affair with a Dominican pop sensation. To make matters worse, he tore the anterior cruciate ligament in his right knee playing an alley cat in a music video for his girlfriend. She dumped him while he was still in surgery. He still pulls in $5 million a movie, though, so you might as well ask him.

"Hey, Dylan, I think we may have met before. Maybe at Ahmet Ertegun's after party at the Grammys? I'm the CEO of Fleece."

"Sure, sure," he says. "Do you have any free clothes for me?"

"I have just the thing for you if you can give me some financial advice," you respond. "I've got a pretty simple question. Where does someone put ten million when they want it to be liquid but still earn a healthy return?"

"Oh, that's easy," says Dylan. "Terry Ciccone. He manages portfolios for tons of actors, as well as a couple of jam bands. His company is called Pandora Investments. Last year he doubled my money, and when I wanted to take it out

to buy a house in Bridgehampton for me and . . ." His eyes
glaze over. "Anyway, it wasn't a problem."

5 ↑1.75 ADLAC 22 ↓2.60 ENE 50.50 ↑1.50 TYC 60.25 ↓1.75 MSO 65 ↑2.50

*Do you take the advice of an actor—whose last starring role was as
a New York City detective who was also a genie—and invest with this
guy Ciccone? Go to page 118.*

*Or do you stop star-fucking and do what you were planning to do:
ask the advice of your investment banker? Go to page 114.*

You lead him out the door and down the hall to your office. Fawn looks up at you. "Barry has been calling repeatedly while you were in your meeting. He wants you to call him as soon as you can."

"He doesn't have to worry," you say. "We'll be calling him soon enough." You picture Barry in a bright orange prison jumpsuit—maybe working on a chain gang—and a smile comes to your face. "Fawn, hold all calls. No interruptions whatsoever."

Fawn nods and sits down at her desk, watching as you and Flaxworthy march into your office like two executioners. As you close the door behind you, you find Weiss sleeping like a baby on your couch.

"This is your accountant?" Flaxworthy asks.

You nod. "Weiss, wake up. We need to talk to you."

Weiss wakes up startled and confused. It only takes a second, though, for him to remember that he's in your office and why he's there. He looks at Flaxworthy and an expression of sheer terror grips his face. His sits up straight.

Flaxworthy joins him on the couch. "Hello, Mr. Weiss, my name is Jerry Flaxworthy. I work in the regulatory division of the SEC. Your boss has told me about what's going on and I'm here to help you, but only if you help us."

Weiss looks at Flaxworthy and then back at you. Suddenly he turns beet red and explodes. "This is a trap!" he yells, jumping from the couch. "You're trying to put this all on me! I was trying to help this company, and the first thing you do is call the cops? What the hell?" Weiss scurries behind your desk.

"Jerry's not a cop, Weiss," you say, trying to calm him down. "This guy is not after you. But you have to cooperate and come clean so that we can get out of this mess."

"I'm not going to jail because I was doing what I could to save this piece of shit place. My wife—"

Flaxworthy cuts in, "We want Moneyhouse, not you. If you

work with us, you can get a reduced sentence or possibly no jail time at all."

"Moneyhouse!" Weiss exclaims. "You want me to testify against Moneyhouse? He killed Stonecutter—everyone knows that! This is some deal; either get knifed in prison or be found washed up on the shores of the Hudson."

Out of the blue, a wave of serenity washes over his face. "Wait, I'll take the third option." He's wearing a thousand-yard gaze. "The third option," he whispers to himself. "Yeah, there is always a third way. . . . I always liked you, boss." And with that, Weiss turns from your desk and starts moving toward the window.

The windows in your building are sealed for climate control. But if Weiss gets enough speed, he could easily break through and fall the thirteen stories to his death.

He steps back as if he's a place kicker marking out his routine and then runs full speed toward the window. You dive, grabbing his jacket to try and hold him back. He spins around in an attempt to knock you loose, but his move is so violent, it snaps you right past him.

You slam against what you hope is the wall, with the full weight of Weiss on top of you. You close your eyes, expecting to hear the sound of glass breaking, but the crash never comes. *Thank God we missed the window*, you think.

Before you've finished the thought, you open your eyes and realize that you're looking into your office from the outside, thirteen stories up in the air. There was no broken glass because the whole window popped out.

The next thing you see is Weiss looking down at you, and Flaxworthy's head poking out over his shoulder.

I don't believe this, you think as you start to pick up speed.

The end

To whom it may concern,

    I have done a very bad thing, something that would probably send me to jail for a long time. But I did it to save the company I love and the reputation of the man I respect more than anyone else. I respected him so much that I did his bidding and transgressed moral and ethical boundaries that I would not have done alone. I'm too ashamed to face my family or the people of this company, but I think the final favor I can do for them is to expose the decay that runs through this company, all the way to the top. My boss believes in Fleece—he believes that sportswear can be more than fashion, that it can facilitate a better way of life. All of his good intentions, however, were slowly being corroded by his desire for money and power. He knew that being a public company would make him richer than any product he could create. He forced Barry and me to hide rising costs and forge profits for the sake of attracting investors. He told me to cook the books; he even gave me the recipe.

    The key that you found on the top of this note is the key to my filing cabinet. In there you will find all the documentation of our elaborate fraud—every page approved by my boss.

    I'm sorry for what I did, and I now know that I can never face my family or society with anything but shame again.

Adieu,
Larry Weiss

All you want to do is leave your office and go home. You look out the broken window and it seems like the best way to go.

The end

"Actually, Felix, why don't you do this? Sell about half of Barry's shares along with mine. Get on it right now. I've got a meeting with him in a few minutes. I'll let him know."

"Wait," says Felix. "What the hell is going on here? I can't sell his shares without his okay. I need to call him."

"Do that and you're fired," you say. "I'll take all my money and send it down to Carlucci in DC. You don't want me to do that, do you, Felix? After all, what's the commission on a seventy-million-dollar trade? A million bucks? That could buy you a place in the Hamptons. I'm going to tell Barry as soon as I see him. I just want him hearing it from me, and not you."

Felix, ever the Wall Streeter, puts his own financial well-being ahead of his client's and agrees to do what you've told him.

You hang up, dial Fawn, and tell her to get Barry back in your office. He arrives with the same look on his face as he had when he left.

"Barry, sit down." He does. "You and I are going to write our resignation letters right now," you say.

"Resign? What the hell are you talking about?"

"Barry, get your head out of your ass. Our T-shirts don't work. Like you said, Fleece is fucked. And so is our stock. I've instructed Felix to sell two hundred and fifty thousand of your shares and five million of mine. Here's how we're going to play this. We'll resign tomorrow, claiming surprise at the news. If anyone asks us about the shares, we talked at lunch today and decided Fleece was richly valued. Who's going to tell on us? Not our little friend in the office of the Joint Chiefs. And let me tell you something. It's not going to be any fun working here after this news breaks. We might as well take a well-deserved vacation."

Barry breaks into a broad smile. "This is why I like working with you," he says. "Hand me a piece of paper. My resignation letter will be a real humdinger."

"As will mine," you say. "As will mine."

5 ↑ 1.75 ADLAC 22 ↓ 2.60 ENE 50.50 ↑ 1.50 TYC 60.25 ↓ 1.75 MSO 65 ↑ 2.50

Go to page 113.

You are arrested with the help of the man who put you in the mess in the first place.

All your life you tried to create a positive image of yourself as hardworking and honest. You lived the straight and narrow for your whole career and only got modest press in trade and outdoor magazines. But now that you have erred, you realize that leading a good life is a boring news story. No news is good news, and bad news sells papers:

 October 29:

CEO FLEECES INVESTORS

 November 10:

MONEYHOUSE OF CARDS

NEW YORK OBSERVER November 12:

BULLETPROOF NO MORE

 November 18:

ATTORNEY GENERAL CRAVEN ALBANIE FINDS FLEECE NOT SO GOLDEN

THE WALL STREET JOURNAL. November 22:

FLEECE UNRAVELS

The New York Times December 10:

JUDGE SIZES UP CLOTHING MAGNATE. FINDS SEVEN TO TEN BEST FIT

The end

The next morning you're chomping on your cinnamon raisin bagel at your desk and reading the latest injury report of the Yankees' star Cuban pitcher when you hear loud talking and music coming from beyond your office door.

You get up and open your door to find that Carson Rodriguez has arrived. He's leaning on Fawn's desk, holding her necklace close to his face.

"Jade was created by the earth to rest on your neck." Carson has Fawn captivated. *I thought this guy was gay*, you think as you wait for Carson to acknowledge your presence.

Carson turns to you, salutes, and releases Fawn's necklace. "Private Benjamin reporting for duty here in Tragic-istan. Seriously, honey, this office is a dump."

He is gay.

"How do any of you get work done around here? It's like working in a factory in East Berlin. Let's go into your office and try to resurrect the dead!"

Carson blows past you into your office. As your office door closes you hear him shriek, "Oh my God! A boulder would go perfectly in this corner!"

For the next week and a half you work out of the conference room as Carson resuscitates your office. He has ordered you not to look until it is finished, but you've seen some of the daily deliveries arriving. Enormous paintings, a chaise longue, a bubble-wrapped bidet, a globe that doubles as a bar, something that looks like a stuffed horse, and a boulder craned in through your office window. (You watched that happen from the sidewalk when you went out for a hot dog.)

In addition to being the city's premier interior decorator, Carson is a fountain of unsolicited advice. He has a sarcastic remark at the ready on everything from your latest business clothing line for men ("Steve Guttenberg called—he wants his lapels back.") to your women's après-ski designs ("I didn't know lesbian robots went skiing.")

Carson finishes just in time for you to pose for the *Ivy Business Review*. You don't recognize your office—it looks like the office of a corporate emperor, with all the luxuries to relax your soul when the problems of the world are on your mind. And you love it. So does the magazine's photographer, who can't stop marveling about your new desk, which is complex in its minimalism. You're sitting on the edge of it, as instructed, when a woman pushes open the door of your office. The shot they end up using in the magazine is one of you staring not at the camera, but at her. She's beautiful.

Go to page 117.

Six days after the quarter's end, you're due to meet with your chief financial officer, Alan Baldacker, to get the postmortem on what most certainly will be the worst three months Fleece has had as a public company—if not in its entire existence. But again, you're secure in the knowledge that things can't get any worse than they've already been.

The only problem: You underestimated just how bad things had gotten.

"We lost six key accounts in California, Asian sales are off because of currency turmoil caused by that hedge fund guy Gord Boros, and we're experiencing an unprecedented level of returns because of the shipping problems we had," says Baldacker. "We're going to miss our projections by fifty percent."

Fifty percent? Your stock will be crushed when you release the news. The cycle of positive reinforcement that worked on the way up might even turn into a negative one on the way down. It's not uncommon for negative stories in the financial press to make the jump over to the fashion pages—the results of that could be devastating.

"Unless . . . ," Baldacker continues.

"Unless what? How do we whitewash a disaster of this magnitude? Unless what, Baldacker?"

"Unless you think an accounting maneuver I've come across would get by our auditors." He hands you a sheet of paper with several different calculations on it.

Baldacker then explains his idea to you. If you change the way that Fleece accounts for the cost overruns in the quarter related to the returned clothes, you could boost Fleece's pretax income by 46.1 percent, to $278.8 million, effectively wiping out the shortfall. Best of all, it's legal.

You want to hug Baldacker, but you restrain yourself. You knew this guy was good, but you had no idea he was *this* good. Finding a loophole—and a legal one at that—in the eleventh hour may just save your company. You hate to deceive your auditors and investors, but sometimes one must lie to protect them. It's either that or sitting back and watching as your future gets flushed down the toilet.

15 ↑ 1.75 ADLAC 22 ↓ 2.60 ENE 50.50 ↑ 1.50 TYC 60.25 ↓ 1.75 MSO 65 ↑ 2.

Do you do what Baldacker suggests, and make the accounting change? Go to page 168.

Or do you instead face the consequences of Fleece's—and your own— missteps during the quarter, and tell Wall Street what really happened to your business? Go to page 110.

That evening when you walk into your apartment on Riverside Drive and Ninety-fifth Street, your wife is there with a short man whose head is shaved except for a Manchu ponytail, wearing a tight black T-shirt and three-thousand-dollar jeans.

"Honey, you know Carson Rodriguez. His ideas for the apartment are truly inspired."

"Of course. Carson's a genius, or so he tells me," you say, thinking back to your phone conversation with him. "Will it be terra-cotta for the home as well?"

"Don't belittle what you don't understand," he says, and turns his back to you, grabbing your wife's arm. He points to where the refrigerator is and says, "This is your integrity corner. You need weight there. That's where we'll put the boulder."

"A refrigerator isn't heavy?" you ask with more than a hint of sarcasm.

"Honey, don't belittle what you don't understand," says your wife.

This is ridiculous. You turn to leave. "I guess I'll understand it when I see the invoice," you say.

Before you can retreat to your den, Rodriguez says, "That's a good point. Do you want me to just add these renovations to the tab we're running in your office?"

5 ↑ 1.75 ADLAC 22 ↓ 2.60 ENE 50.50 ↑ 1.50 TYC 60.25 ↓ 1.75 MSO 65 ↑ 2.50

Do you tell him to bill your home decor to Fleece? Go to page 158.
Or do you keep things separate, and pay your own bills? Go to page 161.

You're sitting at the bar of the St. Regis Hotel sipping on a glass of Johnnie Walker Blue. It's 2:00 in the afternoon, and normally you wouldn't be sneaking in a drink in the middle of the day. But this is not a normal day. You are about to go upstairs to your quarterly analyst meeting and break the bad news to the Wall Street community about Fleece's disastrous quarter. You gulp back the last of the scotch, push yourself away from the bar, and head into the hotel lobby, walking like a man headed toward the executioner.

Within two minutes of your speech to the analysts, they are no longer listening to you. All they needed to hear from you was "missed projections by fifty percent," and everybody had their heads down punching away at their BlackBerrys or ducking out the door to call their firms' brokers and tell them to sell, sell, sell! Before you have even finished your report, the bad news is already front-page news on every financial Web site.

That afternoon you're back in your office watching CNBC. You assumed your stock would drop about 50 percent, in line with the failed projections, but in fact it's plunged to the dark depths of a single-digit stock price. The last trade of the day initiates Fleece shares into the infamous club of penny stocks, trading hands at just ninety-seven cents apiece.

Your own stake in the company is now worth a paltry $9.7 million. When you get home, you follow the sounds of hysterical sobbing to your master bathroom, where you find your wife in the bathtub with streaks of mascara running down her cheeks.

"We're ruined!" she screams at you as if you had no idea what was going on. "You should have made the soldiers those T-shirts! Apple will have to change schools!"

"Honey, we'll get through this, but I need you to be strong. It's just money; we still have each other."

"We'll have each other all right. But that's it. No friends. No life!"

"What has happened to you?" you scream. "Snap out of it! I

made all this money and I'll do it again! Don't be such a selfish bitch!"

Apple pops her head into the bathroom just in time to hear you call her mother a bitch.

"Dad, Mr. Carlucci is on the phone for you. Shall I tell him to call you back?"

You hope Fred is not calling you to tell you that he didn't sell any of your Fleece stock. "No, I'll talk to him right now."

You pick up the phone in your den. "I got it, Apple, you can hang up."

"Dad, I want to switch schools," Apple says over the phone.

"Apple, hang up the phone."

Apple hangs up the phone. And Carlucci begins, "I hope you're wearing your Silk Armor today, because I betcha there are a lot of investors out gunning for you!" Carlucci always prided himself on his amazing sense of humor, but unfortunately no one ever agreed with him.

"You better not be calling me to tell me that you haven't had time to sell my stock."

"Actually, that's why I'm calling. My new assistant—she's cute, but not very effective—left to go skiing before getting the sale in. That ten million you gave me is worth about five grand."

"I can't believe this! That was all I had left! You screwed me!"

"Ha-ha! You New Yorkers are more gullible than your reputation. When someone from Washington tells you something, never believe it. Obviously I got rid of the stock. You're fine. Actually, your ten mil has gained a few hundred thou, but that's not why I'm calling. If you calm yourself down, I have a proposal for you."

"Look, Carlucci. I don't have time for this right now. I have a hysterical wife sitting in the bathtub, a daughter who wants to drop out of school, and stock trading for under a buck. Can't this wait?"

"No, it can't," he replies. "In fact, that stock price is exactly what I want to talk to you about. I was golfing with C. Hoone Dickens this afternoon, and he suggested that this might be an optimal time for you to do a management buyout and take Fleece private again. After all, you haven't exactly been a stand-out performer as a public company. And you're never going to see a deal like this on Fleece stock again. Listen, I believe in you. And I believe in Fleece. You could make a fortune. And Dickens is willing to kick in as much money as you need to get the deal done."

"Take Fleece private? We just went public!"

"Right. And look at the mess you're in. It's the smart thing to do. And Dickens won't be interested in this for long. You've got to decide before he loses interest."

15 ↑1.75 ADLAC 22 ↓2.60 ENE 50.50 ↑1.50 TYC 60.25 ↓1.75 MSO 65 ↑2.5

Go to page 31.

Your letter is a wonderful work of fiction:

> To the Fleece family:
> Effective immediately, I will step down as the chief executive officer of Fleece Industries. I leave the post with mixed emotions. I founded this company more than twenty years ago and have watched it grow to a wondrous behemoth that clothed a generation. But I feel that Fleece can now discover its own direction as a true force in American commerce.
> I leave, simply, because I have reached a stage in my life where I would like to spend more time with my wife and daughter, where I can look deeper into myself and discover what else I have to contribute to the world, and finally where I can wear the clothes that I worked so hard to create where they're truly meant to be worn: the great outdoors.
> Fleece flourished because we performed as a team. Selflessness, compassion, and cooperation paved the path to success for us. As a result we have become winners together, celebrating in the good times and uniting when times got tough. And so I leave you with Fleece. A company built on hard work and decent values. I leave you a company that is strong, tenacious, and brimming with endless possibilities.
> I leave you with the future.
> Sincerely,
> Your (former) CEO

Barry's letter is a little more direct:

Gone sailing.
  —Barry

The end

You politely thank Starr for the information and tell him you'll have a couple of tear-away suits sent to his agent's office. "They're a godsend for people with nagging injuries who find it difficult just to get undressed," you explain. He just stares back at you with the same blank look on his face that he has in every single one of his movies.

After a few weeks of interviewing personal investment managers your investment banker had recommended to you, you ultimately decide to place your money with Sniggs Bank, a DC-based operation that also runs money for the Saudis and Augusto Pinochet.

It's at a lunch in Washington with Fred Carlucci, your new money manager, that you make an acquaintance who will change the direction of Fleece's business forever. You've just finished explaining to him that you want him to sell the $10 million stock grant that you received from the board to diversify your portfolio. You figure you already have enough Fleece stock as it is.

"Of course. Good idea. I'll get right on it," he says, signaling the waiter over by shaking his scotch tumbler.

The two of you are enjoying filet mignon at Bobby Van's Steakhouse when Ralph Kove, a close adviser to the president, walks up to the table.

Fred jumps up. "Ralph, how are you? I haven't seen you since that party at the veep's house in May! This is the CEO of Fleece Industries, by the way. A new client."

You stand up and shake hands with Kove. "Fleece . . . the bulletproof stuff?" he says, not really looking at you but seeming to scan the room for anybody more important.

"Yes, that's right," you respond. "And windproof, waterproof, and fireproof."

"Not much water in Iraq," he says, and then turns to Carlucci. "Fred, the president's father is having a little get-together next week with a few heads of state in hopes of putting together a consortium to build a wireless network in China. You might want to be there. Have you had a background check done recently?"

"Yes, I have, and yes, I'll be there," says Carlucci, shaking hands with Kove before he walks away.

"What did he mean by 'Not much water in Iraq'?" you ask Carlucci when you've both sat down again.

"He means Iraq is a desert," he says. "The man doesn't say anything that doesn't connect back to POTUS. Clearly you're now on his radar."

↑ 1.75 ADLAC 22 ↓ 2.60 ENE 50.50 ↑ 1.50 TYC 60.25 ↓ 1.75 MSO 65 ↑ 2.50

Go to page 83.

Everything goes according to plan on Monday morning as well. Fleece stock bounces *past* where it had been before the news broke—you tell yourself you'll never understand investors—before leveling off by the afternoon.

It occurs to you that you wish you hadn't called Felix and told him to sell the shares. Oh well, you can always just buy back Fleece stock in the open market. You'll only be out the commission the little bastard takes on each transaction.

Fawn comes into your office with a vase full of flowers. "Somebody sent these with a note saying, 'Thanks for keeping an eye out for our kids.' It wasn't even signed. Oh, also CNN called and asked whether you could drop by their offices at six thirty tonight for an interview on the show with Hugh Cobbs."

"I can't, Fawn. You know that. I have a dinner meeting at six with those new subcontractors to talk to them about their taking over the Bangalore contract. Tell Barry to go. He loves getting in front of the camera. If CNN balks, tell them I promise to come by again if they take Barry today."

You spend the rest of the day fielding calls from reporters, explaining your heartfelt sympathy for the soldiers' families, your complete shock at the treachery of the Indians, and your wish that Fleece could do more for the families beyond the foundation you are setting up. You bring Claire Illustrado of CNBC to tears when you tell her about the depth of the pain you felt when you found out about the failure of the shirts on Friday.

And since no one seems to have noticed your stock sale on Thursday afternoon, you call Felix and tell him to buy back the shares.

"You're crazy," he says.

"Like a fox, Felix. Like a fox."

E 15 ↑1.75 ADLAC 22 ↓2.60 ENE 50.50 ↑1.50 TYC 60.25 ↓1.75 MSO 65 ↑2

Go to page 125.

A week later you're sitting in a swinging bench on the front porch of the Adirondack Inn with Sally Laufetter, the editor of the *Ivy Business Review*. You're holding cups of local moonshine that you bought from the guy who rented you the cabins for the weekend.

Mere seconds after describing how you had secured a massive government contract—making her promise to keep the part about Kove off the record—she began touching you when asking you questions. And soon the interview degenerated into nothing more than flimsily veiled flirting on both sides.

"So what's your projected growth?" she asks, rubbing your forearm.

"It depends on the economy's stimulation," you reply.

But Sally does actually interview you, coaching you on your answers. She has an amazing mind, and it seems like she has the whole article framed in her brain. She also has a knack for classifying different trees and distinguishing birdcalls.

One thing leads to another, and within a few hours the two of you find yourselves back in her cabin, naked under a hot shower. "You're my Grizzly Adams," she coos.

"And you're my Gentle Eve," you reply, squeezing her apple of an ass.

Later that evening you call your wife to tell her everything is okay up at the inn. "This editor's a real ball breaker, though, I'll tell you that. But I'm impressing her with some stuff about things like 'Six Sigma' and 'unconsciously competent performance.'"

After listening to the inane details of your wife's day, you hang up the phone and look down at Sally's head bobbing up and down in your lap.

5 ↑1.75 ADLAC 22 ↓2.60 ENE 50.50 ↑1.50 TYC 60.25 ↓1.75 MSO 65 ↑2.50

Go to page 182.

You go ahead and ask Starr for Ciccone's phone number and head home for the evening. When you arrive, Apple is sitting in the living room with a few friends watching MTV.

"Hello, my dear," you say to her. "Who have you got here with you?"

"Dad, this is London and Rebecca Marriott. They're friends from school." One of them looks a little familiar to you, as if you've seen her on Page Six or something. But that couldn't be the case—if she's Apple's age, then she's just a child.

"Hi, girls, nice to meet you. Hey, Apple—I ran into Dylan Starr today at my physical therapist's office."

"Eww. He's so yesterday, Dad. And he was dating that skank all last year. I never want to see another one of his movies as long as I live."

"He is cute, though," says London. Or Rebecca. You didn't catch which one was which.

"No way," says your daughter. "He's gross."

"Well," you continue, in a redoubled effort to sound cool. "I'm also going to invest with a guy who manages money for jammy bands."

Apple rolls her eyes. "Jam bands, Dad. Jam bands. And who cares? They're so two years ago. The only people who go to those concerts are potheads and hippies who refuse to admit that they're over fifty. We like Soggy Bisquit and Manson Monroe."

"I heard he's got a really big . . . ," says Rebecca (or London) before remembering that you're in the room.

" . . . guitar," she recovers. You take that as a signal to leave.

"Tell your mother I'll be in the den."

Once you're in the den, you boot up your computer and do a Google search for Terry Ciccone. His company's Web site isn't what you'd expect from a money manager: There are pictures of him partying in Vegas with A-list actors, hanging out with that ridiculous street magician who froze himself solid for thirty days, and sitting in the front row at a Marisa Antoinette concert. You notice that his office is in Soho—an interesting place for a financial firm. You pick up your phone and dial the number Starr gave you.

"Ciccone," says the voice on the other end of the line.

"Hi, Terry, I'm the CEO of Fleece Industries, and Dylan Starr recommended you as a good money manager. I'm about to have ten million dollars burning a hole in my pocket."

After a five-minute conversation he's charmed you into taking him on as the protector of your assets. You tell him that you'll have the stock wired to him as soon as it's hit your brokerage account.

5 ↑ 1.75 ADLAC 22 ↓ 2.60 ENE 50.50 ↑ 1.50 TYC 60.25 ↓ 1.75 MSO 65 ↑ 2.50

Go to page 244.

When you arrive on the fourteenth floor, Fawn is at her desk wiping tears from her eyes.

"Sir, the whole board is on a conference call waiting for you. They're pretty upset."

"I bet they are. Fawn, I need a black coffee and buttered roll immediately. Coffee first." You then walk into your office, drop your Argonauts gym bag on the floor, and get a wet towel to put around your neck. You plop on the sofa and stare at the blinking red light on your phone. You wait until Fawn gets you your coffee and then you pick up the line.

"Gentlemen, I apologize for this. I have no idea how the debt did not make it into the report," you say, sipping your coffee.

"We do," says Clark Henderson, an outside director, in his nasal voice. "Baldacker told us that you ordered him to keep the loan off the books. We thanked him for his honesty and then fired him."

"You don't believe him, do you?"

"Son, don't. We know what happened and we're furious. Don't make us angrier by lying to us." It's Jack Fielding speaking, an old friend and mentor from when you first went into business. You know you've broken his heart. "Obviously we're not going to let you run Fleece anymore. I just hope you don't go to jail. I want you to hear this from me. I'm taking over as CEO."

"I'm glad it's you, Jack." You hang up the phone, and then with a sudden fit of rage you tear it out of the wall and throw it into your bathroom, where it lands in the toilet. "Field goal."

Eighteen months later you are sitting in a luxury box at Crocodile Field in Jacksonville, Florida, watching the Argonauts roll over the San Diego Sharks in the Super Bowl. Your wife and Apple are with you, as is Tyree Stubbs, who's going crazy. Apparently he bet against your team. Jack Fielding is your guest as well.

The fallout from the hidden loan was minimal. You settled

an investigation with the Securities and Exchange Commission "without admitting or denying guilt" and only had to pay a nominal fine of five thousand dollars and accept a lifelong ban from acting as an executive of a publicly traded company. You even got to keep ownership of the team after working out an arrangement with Fielding and the Fleece board whereby they would continue to guarantee the loan you took to buy the Argonauts, in exchange for season tickets for every member of the board.

The last play of the game is on the Sharks' 45-yard line. Your kicker nails a 55-yard shot through the uprights, sealing the victory.

"Field goal!" you say to Apple. She can't hear you. She's listening to her iPod.

The end

You steel yourself for the fury of a woman scorned.

"Oh, Tiffany, I don't think that would work. What would my wife think? What would they say in the office? We had a great time, you and me, but there must be a better way for you to get yourself on TV than through some bit part in a reality show."

You stop there, knowing that if this plan is going to backfire, you've already said enough. Plus, the security guard has turned down his portable television and is quite clearly listening to you.

Instead of going off-kilter, Tiffany merely deflates. "I guess you're right," she says, her shoulders slumping. "I just got so desperate, and even though you weren't that good in the sack, I thought maybe I could suffer through a few more hours of your grunting and panting if I could get on network television."

"Tiffany, I don't know if you've noticed, but I've been working out . . . ," you start to say, and then stop yourself. She's agreeing with you!

"I'm pretty good in bed," says the guard.

"Shut the hell up or I'll have you fired," you say to him, and grab Tiffany by the arm. "Come with me—I think I know someone who can help you."

You lead Tiffany into the makeshift office that the network has set up for you at the studio. You point to a bar stool sitting in the middle of the room, and Tiffany sits down on it. You pick up the phone and call Fawn. "Fawn, can you get me Stu Kovacs's number? I've got someone I want him to meet."

Tiffany almost falls off the stool. "Stu Kovacs! *The* Stu Kovacs? Oh my God! Oh my God! I've wanted to meet him forever. But to work for him? Oh my God."

Fawn comes back on the line and gives you the number. "Oh, one more thing," she says. "The police were by today. Apparently Tyree Stubbs has been arrested for groping some woman on a cruise ship. And someone told them that he'd tried something similar at a party in Los Angeles. They got a list of people who were there, and for some reason, they think *you* were at his house that night. I told them that you're so square, there's no way you would be at a party like that, but they want you to call them. Want the number?"

"Sure," you say. "But I have no idea what they're talking about. . . ."

Go to page 133.

Your wife, it turns out, was at Fawn's apartment the whole time she was "missing." As sometimes happens in such scenarios, the two women scorned find they have a lot in common. First and foremost, they both hate you more than anyone. Page Six catches them sharing a few drinks at the Oak Bar at the Plaza, and the candid photo makes them look like childhood friends.

But they hadn't been spending their time merely commiserating. Instead, they were poring over Fleece documents that Fawn had made off with the day she left. And when the details of your $10 million stock grant reach the public, you become the whipping boy for an era of over-the-top greed. You are ousted by a breakaway group of Fleece board members led by Ken Hart.

But the embarrassment doesn't stop there. Fawn had also kept documents regarding your retirement agreement, and the tabloids have a field day with the perks: your tab at Jean Georges, a box at Madison Square Garden, VIP tickets to the Olympics, country club dues, and even an allotment for toiletries, vitamins, and flowers. The shocker, which turns New York City against you forever, are season tickets to the Red Sox. Fleece ultimately voids the agreement.

In a virtuoso performance of shock, Sally Laufetter flees into the arms of Ken Hart and eventually marries him.

The end

The next morning you're sitting in your office when there's a knock at the door. Barry bounces in with a videotape in his hand.

"You shoulda seen me, boss. I was on fire. I nailed every question, and even sparred a little with the Secretary of the Treasury, who was there defending outsourcing. I told him he should tell that to the parents of those soldiers."

"Well, put it in the VCR, then," you say. "I can't wait to see it."

Barry pops it in and fast-forwards through the host's opening monologue until his own face appears on screen.

". . . and we were shocked, quite shocked," he says. "We immediately started testing the shirts, and—"

The host interrupts him. "And when was this again?"

"Thursday afternoon," says Barry. "So, as I was saying, we had the shirts tested, and . . ."

You're out of your chair and grabbing the remote out of his hands before he realizes what's going on.

"What the—?" he says.

"What day did you just say, Barry? What day? Did I hear you say Thursday? I think I heard you say Thursday. . . ."

You rewind the tape and replay it. Thursday. The idiot said Thursday.

"Jesus, Barry."

"Oh man," he says. "I'm sorry. Oh, I'm sorry . . . wait. What difference does it make? Sure, we pretended not to know in advance, but why does it matter, anyway?"

You remember that Barry doesn't know about your selling the shares. And you've got to get into your electronic calendar and delete that "urgent" meeting he had with you. If anyone starts snooping around, they'd bust you for insider trading without batting an eye. You kick him out of your office without further explanation, sit down at your desk, and pull up your calendar.

You delete the meeting.

And then you have second thoughts. They know when people make changes to these things, don't they?

15 ↑1.75 ADLAC 22 ↓2.60 ENE 50.50 ↑1.50 TYC 60.25 ↓1.75 MSO 65 ↑2

Do you call your self-righteous IT department and ask them to help you "undelete" the meeting with Barry? Go to page 176.

Or do you just leave it as is, in hopes that any investigation—which is unlikely anyway—won't be so serious that they actually find out about the deletion? Go to page 15.

"You can leave your stuff in here," you say as the two of you stand up. "No thieves in this operation." *What am I doing?* you ask yourself. *Bend it, don't break it.*

Just then Flaxworthy's cell phone rings. "I've got to take this," he says. You nod and stay where you are. "Um, could I actually have a little privacy?" he asks.

"Of course, what was I . . . of course, sorry," you say, and walk toward the glass conference room door. You step out into the hallway and softly pull it closed behind you.

You're at a loss for what to do with yourself. You don't want to just walk away, but there's nothing to busy yourself with in the hallway except a large ficus plant and a painting of a sheep dressed like Superman—a watercolor you found in Haight-Ashbury years ago that seemed symbolic of Fleece's mission to you at the time . . . though that could have had something to do with the "brownie" you'd eaten that day.

You look back into the conference room. Flaxworthy is pacing back and forth. He looks up at you. You nod to him. He nods back and looks down. He walks across the room and then looks up at you again. You nod again. Suddenly it occurs to you: *Is Flaxworthy just looking at me? Or is he looking at me?* He's now staring straight at you and talking into his phone. *He's clearly talking about me,* you think.

All at once sweat starts spritzing into your clothes like a lawn sprinkler on a fairway.

Go to page 190.

You turn to Sutinis. "May I sit at my own desk, please? Unless, of course, you're still busy rifling through my drawers."

"Don't get snippy. We're here to help," she says. "We've got to nip this in the bud. It wasn't me who told you to go spend fifteen thousand dollars on an umbrella stand. And what's this about decorating a hotel room at the Pierre? That's just ridiculous."

"Something on the side, hey?" says Moneyhouse, looking at you as if the two of you are fraternity brothers.

The mood lightens.

"Listen," says Sutinis. "We're not telling you that you have to pay for all these extravagances. It's just that if we're going to do this right, we've got to put a system in place so that we never end up in a situation where someone who wants to bring us down has a smoking gun. You're not running a storefront boutique anymore. This is a public company, and you've got to learn how the shell games are played."

She looks down at your desk and picks up a piece of paper with several different colored boxes on it. "I've prepared a crib sheet for you to use when coding all your future expenses. It even includes that mistress of yours." She holds it out to you. You look over at Moneyhouse. He nods.

15 ↑1.75 ADLAC 22 ↓2.60 ENE 50.50 ↑1.50 TYC 60.25 ↓1.75 MSO 65 ↑2

Do you take the crib sheet from Sutinis and embark on a career of inflated expense accounts and company-paid extramarital affairs? Go to page 45.

Or do you do the right thing and offer to pay for all your own expenses, keeping Fleece out of your private matters? Go to page 147.

As you're pulling up your pants, Diane jumps up off the bed and says, "Let's do it. Let's go to the bank right now."

"Honey, we can't go now. Your hair is . . . all messed up." She leans down, picks your baseball hat up off the floor, puts it on her head, and says, "I'll be fine. Let's go. I don't have all day."

The two of you leave the Pierre and walk to her bank on Park Avenue. She keeps trying to hold your hand on the way, but you know you can't, not yet, not in public. In fact, you're a little nervous, considering how close you are not only to your office but also to your teenage daughter Apple's school. Soon enough, though, you're in the bank and the papers are drawn. It's time to sign.

"I feel like we're signing our marriage certificate," Diane gushes. The banker, who is doing his best to remain anonymous behind his wire-rimmed glasses, looks at you quickly before turning away and shuffling some random papers on his desk.

"Right . . . ," you answer, searching for something else to say. You've got to get out of here and ditch Diane before anybody sees you. Marriage? What the hell were you thinking? You can't marry Diane. You already have a wife and a family, and a reputation that depends on both of those things. "Let's just sign these papers and get out of here," you say.

Diane pauses and looks up at you. A look of anger flashes across her face. "You *are* leaving your wife, right? You just said you would back in the hotel room. Before I sign this, I need you to say it again."

The bank clerk starts shuffling madly and pulls open a drawer in his desk as if he's looking for something. Jesus, you're going to have to pay this guy off as well.

"Diane, not now. Not here. Just sign it. We can talk about this later."

She looks at you, realizing that you're never going to marry her. You know this. She knows this. It's time to take action.

"Diane, let's go outside."

5 ↑ 1.75 ADLAC 22 ↓ 2.60 ENE 50.50 ↑ 1.50 TYC 60.25 ↓ 1.75 MSO 65 ↑ 2.50

Go to page 230.

"Look, Desmond, I appreciate the opportunity, but I really don't think that's the kind of business I want to get into at the moment," you say. "I read the papers—I know what kinds of salaries these people are demanding. I was wondering the other day whether there are *any* sports teams that make a profit anymore. While I'd love the box seats and cheerleaders and all, I just don't think it's the right time."

Just as you couldn't have guessed what Wolfe was going to propose at lunch, you never could have guessed what would come next: He bursts out with a loud bawling, as tears explode from his eyes. Everyone who wasn't already staring at the two of you is now looking your way. Christ!

"Look, Desmond, calm down," you say, instinctively reaching over to wipe the tears off his face, and then realizing what it must look like. "I mean, it's not the end of the world or anything. Surely there's someone out there who'll buy the team. Some software executive or something."

"I *LOVED* him!" he says, much too loudly, and then covers his face in his hands and continues crying. You manage to calm him down by giving him your wineglass, which he empties with one gulp.

After what seems like an endless wait for the check, you finally make it out of the restaurant. You go for a short walk to clear your head and to reassure yourself that you made the right decision. You are not in the business of buying sports teams. You run a clothing company. You save lives with bulletproof clothing—you don't put them in jeopardy by asking big brutes to put on equipment and smash into one another at top speed.

You get back to your office around 2:00 P.M. and launch your Web browser. You want to see whether Chatter.com, the city's main gossip site, has a story yet about seeing you in the restaurant with Wolfe. And they do, with the headline: A BUM DEAL?

You're chuckling softly to yourself when you look at your

electronic calendar. There's a request from Barry McTeagle, your in-house counsel, asking for a meeting as soon as possible. "It's urgent. Extremely," says the message. You send him an instant message telling him to come by now. A few minutes later he walks in, with a look on his face that you've never seen before. *He looks like someone just died*, you think.

You were right.

Go to page 142.

It's December 26, and you're walking back into Henri Bendel. Naturally, your daughter Apple hated the hat you'd bought her, even though it cost six hundred dollars and was exactly what she'd asked for. After a brief confrontation with the store manager, who refuses to give you a refund because you bought the hat more than two weeks ago, you settle for a gift certificate and head back out onto the street.

You walk down to Times Square, thinking you can get Apple something at the MTV store as a replacement for the hat. You end up buying her a biography of Ruben Studdard and a poster of Carson Daly.

As you're making your way up the street, you notice, for the first time, a huge billboard with your face on it and HARRY NEW YEAR AND MANY MORE! written underneath it. Next to you on the sign is a bear wearing a party hat and uncorking a bottle of champagne. You wish they'd taken a better picture of you, but hey, not everybody gets their face plastered on a sign in the crossroads of the world.

You're shaken out of your reverie by someone shouting, "Get out of the way!" You turn and notice a cab squealing toward an elderly Hispanic woman, its brakes locked and its wheels sliding through the black slush. The woman is frozen in her tracks, paralyzed by fear. You're close enough that you might be able to push her out of the way, but you'd also run the risk of being hit by the cab yourself.

15 ↑1.75 ADLAC 22 ↓2.60 ENE 50.50 ↑1.50 TYC 60.25 ↓1.75 MSO 65 ↑2.5

Do you try to save the woman, putting your own charmed life in jeopardy? Go to page 87.

Or do you save your own skin, and let the old boot fend for herself? Go to page 55.

You call Kovacs first so you can get rid of Tiffany. He promises to meet her upon her return to LA, and she leaves Queens in a cloud of excitement, even apologizing for telling you that you didn't have much skill between the sheets. ("I was angry—I didn't really mean it. Well, not all of it.") You don't care. One complication taken care of. But what the hell is going on with Stubbs?

You can't remember much about that night, but you do recall a gaggle of starlets being in the room when you were watching Tiffany partake of the white gold. You hope that won't get out in any of the police interviews. "What happens in Stubby's house stays in Stubby's house," is what Tyree has always said. Apparently that doesn't hold true in his case anymore. You can only hope it does in yours. You decide to hold off on calling the police until you can make sure you haven't forgotten anything.

When you get back to the office in the afternoon, Fawn can barely contain herself. "Page Six called! Page Six called! Some reporter named Ian wants to talk to you about that party at Tyree Stubbs's house. I can't believe you were there, you liar! What's it like? Does he have a hot tub? I bet he has a pet tiger. I read in *Us Weekly* that everyone is getting one."

You aren't sure what to say, but you're suddenly gripped with panic—this could ruin everything! The audience of *The Simple Stitch* skews toward females, for obvious reasons, and those women are unlikely to be impressed that you were at a party where an alleged sexual assault took place.

"I dropped by his place when I was out in LA in October to drop off some clothes," you explain to Fawn. "I guess there might have been a party going on, but I didn't stay. I just gave him the clothes and his endorsement check and went back to my hotel to do some work."

"Oh," says Fawn, obviously disappointed with your apparent lack of knowledge about the inside of an NBA star's house. "Well, okay, here's the number for Ian at Page Six."

5 ↑ 1.75 ADLAC 22 ↓ 2.60 ENE 50.50 ↑ 1.50 TYC 60.25 ↓ 1.75 MSO 65 ↑ 2.50

Go to page 65.

Two years have passed. The Nigerian barge company gathered enough investors to bring your financials back to what you once claimed they were. Fleece has prospered, and you have landed comfortably on the Forbes 400 list of the richest Americans. Six months ago, to your great relief, the barge company mysteriously went under because of a coup d'etat in Nigeria that sank your fleet.

You and your wife are sitting side by side on a dais in the rococo-style ballroom of the Metropolitan Club on Central Park South. She looks lovely in her champagne-colored gown, and you, tanned from your recent weekend playing a couple of rounds at Augusta, look your dapper self in a custom-made Fleece tuxedo. You're tonight's honoree—the recipient of the prestigious Crystal Owl from the Center for Corporate Integrity. The emcee is surprisingly funny as he shoots quick barbs at all the CEOs and former CEOs in the room. He finishes off with a joke about Martha Stewart refusing to wear prison stripes between Labor Day and Memorial Day, and then he introduces you.

"This is the man who designed fireproof athletic gear to prevent flare-ups during his hot streaks. He's the wolf who designed sheep's clothing and survived the ultimate test of going public with strength, leadership, and, most of all, integrity—a true family man and a credit to all you creditors out there. . . . Please help me welcome the youngest, and probably the bravest, of all the Crystal Owl recipients . . . the CEO of Fleece Industries!"

The audience rises to its feet with thunderous applause. At a table nearby, Diane is wiping a tear from her eye as Fawn hands her a tissue. Even the table of previous winners of the Crystal Owl stands. Ivan Boesky, Kenneth Lay, Michael Milken, and Dick Cheney are all on their feet applauding. This is your moment.

You step to the podium. The emcee whispers in your ear that he's wearing Fleece boxers right now, and then punches your shoulder a little too hard. You center yourself, adjust the microphone, and clear your throat.

"It has been a long road—a dangerous road. When I became the CEO of a public company, I was glad I invented bulletproof clothing." (You hold for laughs.) "When one bears an idea into the world and asks others to commit their time and energy to serving that idea, one must go about it with integrity, fidelity, and above all, humility. . . ."

The end

Just as you all finish off the third bottle of champagne, you arrive back at Fleece's corporate offices at 666 Madison Avenue. It's nothing fancy—just a bunch of glass and steel—but the address makes up for the lack of cutting-edge decor. You step through the automatic revolving door and then stand awkwardly as the security staff breaks into a round of applause.

"Thank you . . . thank you," you say to no one in particular, and you look at your watch as an excuse to make your way to the executive elevator. The doors close, and you can finally breathe. You press 14. Like many buildings, yours doesn't have a thirteenth floor. You've often wondered whether merely calling the thirteenth floor the fourteenth floor will protect you from the number's inherent malevolence. But after the morning you've had, superstitions such as these are of little concern.

The elevator doors open and you are greeted by more well-wishing employees giving you a standing ovation. It's no surprise—they've become rich today as well.

You break through the throngs of handshakes and hugs and make your way to your anchor, your girl Friday, Fawn Corridoir. Fawn, your secretary, is a towering six-foot blond plank of wood whose silk blouse reveals more than it hides. You greet her warmly (maybe a little too warmly, but hey, your wife has gone home).

"Only a couple of calls for you," she says, handing you several phone messages.

"Thanks, Fawn." You walk through the open steel double doors to your office and close them behind you.

You take a moment to soak in your office, which suddenly feels a little different to you. On the left is a six-foot-long mustard-colored leather couch. On the right is a long credenza, full of the first line of clothing that came out of the Fleece factory back in 1982. There's an aerodynamic running suit with mesh lapels, magnetic suspenders to attach pins and name tags without puncturing the fabric, climate-controlled leg warmers, and a novelty tuxedo T-shirt that repels cigarette smoke.

You turn and look across the room at the framed photo above the couch. It's you and J. J. Koone. He's your mentor, the creator of the indestructible, impervious Maine Hunting Boot. The inspiration for Silk Armor. He's got his arm around you and is whispering something in your ear. You remember the rustic wisdom he imparted to you that day, something you've never told a soul. "Don't go deeper than the boot goes high," he said. You haven't done so yet, and you don't plan to anytime soon.

As you look down at the messages in your hand, your cell phone rings. It's a number you don't recognize. You almost answer it but then stop youself. You're the CEO of a public company now—you don't take calls from people you don't know. Or do you? It occurs to you that you're about to make your first decision as the CEO of a public company, albeit a fairly innocuous one.

15 ↑ 1.75 ADLAC 22 ↓ 2.60 ENE 50.50 ↑ 1.50 TYC 60.25 ↓ 1.75 MSO 65 ↑ 2.50

Do you answer your cell phone? Go to page 201.

Or do you let the call go to voice mail and read through your messages? Go to page 9.

"Jennifer, I've been wanting to do this since pretty much the day I hired you. You're fired. Get out of my office, and don't come back."

You hit your intercom. "Fawn, have security meet Jennifer at her office and escort her out of the building. Don't let her even touch her computer. And cancel her bonus check."

Jennifer is stunned. It occurs to you that no one has ever spoken to her in this way, and you find yourself enjoying the moment even more than you'd expected.

Later in the day, with Donny Scott's help, you craft the best press release possible under the circumstances, explaining to investors that Fleece is going to come up short this quarter.

The result is predictable: The stock takes a tumble, falling more than 25 percent in one day, and the phones start ringing off the hook.

Over the next few months you are the subject of numerous scathing business stories that describe your rough transition from a private to a public company, and you fall off the invite lists of New York's air-kiss benefits.

It all turns around for you, though, when you receive a call from Terence Southern, the CEO of Yankee Fabric, a $25 billion clothing behemoth. Southern is legendary for picking up smaller companies on the cheap, and he tells you he considers the softness in Fleece stock an incredible buying opportunity. You agree to sell the company and take on the role of a roving ambassador for Fleece, without any real job responsibilities at all.

Over time you sell your stock in Yankee Fabric and plow the proceeds into an increasing number of highly profitable real estate deals. You're out of the CEO business, but you're very, very wealthy. You haven't thought about clothing designs in months, preferring to focus on charting your route as you and your wife sail your yacht through the Mediterranean.

The end

It's the next morning, and you wake up in your office to the sound of Fawn settling in at her desk. You fell asleep in your office brainstorming titles for your new reality show. *Rugged Man, Clothes Horse, Fashion Survivor, I'm a Clothing Designer: Get Me Out of Here!, The Real World of Fleece, Who Wants to Be a Designer?, The Simple Stitch.*

Araz and Jeff are snuggled up on the floor like two kittens keeping each other warm. You sit up on your couch, fighting the stiffness in your back—a stiffness you haven't felt since your wife made you sleep in your office a couple of years ago for drunkenly calling her mother a cunt at Thanksgiving. "Guys. Guys! Wake up, go home, take a shower, and be back by noon."

Your two marketing men slowly regain consciousness and realize that they were cuddling in their sleep. Jeff pushes Araz away from him, and Araz throws Jeff's sneaker at his head. They get up without saying a word and leave the office pushing and shoving each other.

"Morning. Ewww, boy smell," you hear Fawn say as the doors close behind them. You go to your desk and check the Fleece stock price on Yahoo. It hasn't changed since the closing bell, but you like to look at the ticker and remind yourself that you are the CEO of a public company.

Fawn walks in with your cinnamon raisin bagel and cream cheese. "Good morning. Did you guys have a slumber party last night?" she jokes as she puts your bagel and coffee on your desk.

"Yeah, we ate raw cookie dough, talked about boys, and had a pillow fight in our bulletproof jammies." You take a bite of the bagel and slurp some coffee, which spills down your shirt in your groggy state. As you wipe the coffee off your shirt, you notice that you have a little potbelly. It's natural. You're getting older, and the stress of going public has made you eat more. But if you're going to be a reality star, you need to lose some weight.

"Fawn, I'm going to the gym. And no more bagels! I want fruit and bran from now on." You throw the bagel into the trash can and stand up with the gumption of a man on a mission.

"You don't have any gym clothes," Fawn says, picking up beer bottles.

"Fawn, we *make* gym clothes. And I must look good on TV!" You storm out the door and head to the gym with the goal of losing the ten pounds that the camera will mercilessly put on you.

15 ↑1.75 ADLAC 22 ↓2.60 ENE 50.50 ↑1.50 TYC 60.25 ↓1.75 MSO 65 ↑2.

Go to page 197.

The next morning you're up early and in the office by 8:00 A.M. You work through a week's worth of e-mail and phone messages and are pleasantly surprised by the lack of fires to put out. Fleece stock, meanwhile, has trended steadily upward, and press coverage has been glowing.

Fawn comes into your office around 10:15 with an iced coffee and a piece of blueberry buckle cake for you.

"Did *anything* happen while I was gone?" you ask her.

"Not much. This place seems like it's on autopilot. Jennifer Estrangelo was looking for you a couple of times, but other than that, I can't recall anything out of the ordinary. . . . Wait, there was one thing. Donny Scott came by yesterday. He seemed really freaked out about something. But when I told him you were in LA, he said he'd come find you when you got back."

Just then Donny Scott pushes Fawn out of the doorway of your office. Donny is a muscular, perpetually tanned bodybuilder with spiked black hair who works under Jennifer Estrangelo in sales. He always wears clothes one size too small lest you forget that he works out on a daily basis. He is squeezing a rubber stress ball in his hand.

"I'm so glad you're back," he says, walking past her. "Fawn, hold all of his calls for the next half hour."

"That's presumptuous," you say, suddenly quite annoyed with Scott.

"You won't think so after you hear what I have to tell you," he replies.

5 ↑ 1.75 ADLAC 22 ↓ 2.60 ENE 50.50 ↑ 1.50 TYC 60.25 ↓ 1.75 MSO 65 ↑ 2.50

Go to page 80.

"I just got off the phone with a clerk in the office of the Joint Chiefs of Staff," says Barry.

"Really?" you ask. "Do they want us to outfit the marines now? I can totally see them wearing the T-shirts—they are waterproof, after all."

"No, boss, that's not it," he says. "A soldier was killed today in Iraq."

"Did you know him or something? Oh my God, Barry, I'm so sorry. Who was it?"

"No one I know," he replies. "His name was Pat Mayhew. He was from Lancaster, Pennsylvania. . . . He was wearing a Fleece T-shirt. And even though the shooter was about fifty yards away, the bullet went right through the shirt and pierced his heart. This clerk—who says she's a fan of Fleece and wanted to warn us as a way of saying thank you for her Fleece 'Pink Princess' robe that has helped her through many a breakup— told me they're going out with a press release tomorrow about what happened. Fleece is fucked. Totally fucked."

And just like that, the ego that had been expanding for months inside your head deflates. A dead soldier? You realize that not only are you going to hell, but you'll be poor when you get there. Your stock is going to get annihilated tomorrow. Your stock!

"Barry, does anyone else know about this?"

"Not yet. Why?"

"All right. Leave me alone. I have to think."

"Boss, did you hear me? Someone is *dead*."

"I did hear you, Barry," you say, your panic growing. "I'll call you in a couple of minutes."

Barry leaves, shaking his head at your callousness. As soon as your door closes, you reach for your phone, and you start looking for your broker's phone number.

15　↑1.75 ADLAC 22　↓2.60 ENE 50.50　↑1.50 TYC 60.25　↓1.75 MSO 65　↑2.

Do you do call your broker and tell him to start selling your Fleece shares? Go to page 206.

Or do you do the right thing and go down with the ship? Go to page 25.

You tell your cab driver to take you to 69 Wall Street, the legendary address of the Mercantile. After stopping to buy a pack of Alka-Seltzer and some condoms from a corner deli, you arrive downtown forty-five minutes later and see Barry waiting on the sidewalk in front of the club.

"Let's go inside."

"Wait," says Barry, grabbing your arm before you open the door. "There's something I need to talk to you about." He has a weird look on his face. What can be so important that Barry would want to keep Moneyhouse waiting? You start to push open the door, but he stops you again.

"It's about the books. I think we may have a problem," he continues, looking deadly serious.

That stops you in your tracks. What on earth could be wrong with Fleece's books? Larry Weiss, your internal accountant, is as straitlaced a guy as you can get. Doesn't even like music. Barry must be confused about something. He doesn't even deal with the company finances.

"Barry, let's talk about this later," you say, and open the door to the Mercantile.

You were in the Mercantile once before, back in the go-go nineties, when any young punk with an Internet connection and a novel idea, like selling books online, could get Wall Street to hawk their shares to unwitting investors. You remember the interior of the club quite well. Leather chairs, hunting pictures, banquettes with ashtrays full of cigar butts. It's the kind of place that doesn't change with the times—the hallmark of true old-boy exclusivity.

Entering the club, you expected the mood to be more somber, given what the country has been through over the past five years, but you're wrong. When investment bankers take a pay cut, their salaries drop from $10 million to $8.5 million. Still lots of martinis to be bought with that kind of green. As your eyes adjust to the light, you see Moneyhouse sitting under an oil painting of J. P. Moneyhouse III, his grandfather, a notorious stock swindler and contributor to Mussolini. Moneyhouse already has a martini in his hand.

"You're going to need a drink," he says as you sit down, and simultaneously makes a gesture toward what looks to be his own private waiter.

"Sure, I'll have a drink," you say, smiling. But Moneyhouse is not smiling back. *This guy's a stiff,* you think. Barry, for some reason, is rifling through his briefcase. He pulls out a sheaf of papers. As he starts to pass it across the table, you instinctively reach out for it, but instead he hands it to Moneyhouse, who puts it in his own briefcase.

"What the . . . ?" you say.

"Boss, this is what I was trying to tell you," Barry says sheepishly.

"I'll be the one doing the talking from here on in," says Moneyhouse. "Do you realize that Larry Weiss has been cooking the books since the day he got to Fleece? And that you're sitting on top of a fraud of magnificent proportions? To be precise, one-point-five billion dollars. I think you'd better fire your current investment bankers. We're your bankers now. That is, if you want to stay out of the big house. So what do you say? Should we raise a toast to our new partnership?"

You sit back, stunned, and stare at Barry. He can't even look at you. Moneyhouse, on the other hand, hasn't taken his gaze off of you. He's offering you a devil's handshake—you're damned if you do, damned if you don't.

15 ↑1.75 ADLAC 22 ↓2.60 ENE 50.50 ↑1.50 TYC 60.25 ↓1.75 MSO 65 ↑2.

Do you shake hands with Satan? Go to page 205.

Or do you get up, leave the Mercantile, and try to figure out what the hell they're talking about? Go to page 4.

Two days later you're walking into the offices of Moneyhouse and Stonecutter for a meeting with the ten people he has insisted you nominate to the board in addition to yourself and Moneyhouse. You walk through the familiar double doors to an unfamiliar sight. The oaken conference room of Moneyhouse and Stonecutter, usually warm with burgundy leather chairs and soft green table lamps, has an air of steely grey coolness about it. Ten silver-haired businessmen in dark suits surround the desk. They do not greet you warmly. You are not their friend. You are their investment.

You sit down and are about to call the meeting to order when Moneyhouse speaks. "Gentlemen, start your engines. . . ." Everyone laughs, including you. "I have the honor of introducing to you the chairman of Fleece Industries."

"Yes, indeed, start those engines," you say. You're greeted by ten blank stares. "Ahem." You clear your throat. "I'm very excited to meet all of you, of course; you will all be on the slate to be elected at our next shareholder meeting. I am extremely grateful for your interest in Fleece and its bright future." At this point you lean down and lift up the bag you've brought with you and pull out eleven safety orange Fleece crushable hunting hats. "I hope these will come in handy when we're hunting down new opportunities in the years ahead." You push them out into the middle of the table. No one moves. The only thing missing from the stillness of the moment is a tumbleweed rolling across the conference room floor.

Go to page 78.

"Whatever you need, St. James," you say. "You'll need to come to New York tomorrow. I've got a hotel room you can stay in— three eighteen at the Pierre—the money will be waiting for you there. The guy you want to . . . speak to . . . is named Larry Weiss. He lives in a crappy little neighborhood in Brooklyn. He's in the phone book. When it's done, call my office and tell my secretary that the package was delivered. And then don't ever call me again. This is our last conversation. Ever."

"Done," he says, hanging up before you do.

You make your way back to the office, praying that Weiss has actually left for the day in a fit of pique. You're not sure you can handle seeing him again. Luckily Fawn tells you when you get back that Weiss has gone home sick. *He's going to be feeling worse than he does now by sometime tomorrow*, you think. *Hopefully, St. James will make it painless.*

You decide the best course of action will be to go down to the New York Athletic Club and hide in the steam room for the rest of the afternoon. You're feeling dirty anyway.

15 ↑1.75 ADLAC 22 ↓2.60 ENE 50.50 ↑1.50 TYC 60.25 ↓1.75 MSO 65 ↑2.

Go to page 151.

You reach out and take the crib sheet. As you look at the mathematical equations that sum up a series of lies, a chill runs through your bones. *This isn't how I want to do business,* you think. *Hiding a cloned sheep from the government is one thing— it will better our business until legislation catches up to reality—but this is just reckless.*

You hand the paper back to Ms. Sutinis and say, "I'm happy to pay for my own personal luxuries. I'll put all of the non-office Carson Rodriguez expenses on my private gold card. As far as my trip to the Falklands, I'm sure Moneyhouse will understand why Fleece should pay for that flight. That sheep will quadruple our sales. Now, if you don't mind getting your bony ass out of my chair, maybe I can get some work done."

Sutinis looks at Moneyhouse, but he merely shrugs and gets up. Sutinis follows him to the door.

"We're watching you," says Moneyhouse as he picks up his trench coat from the arm of the couch. "We're watching you because we don't want you to fuck up. Good day."

The whole scene leaves you a bit rattled as you sit down to do all the things you have put off for weeks, if not months.

The rest of the day is spent writing thank-you cards, ordering a long-overdue birthday present for Apple, and calling the old folks' home and asking about your mother. You haven't talked to her in years, as she doesn't even recognize you anymore, but it makes you feel better to know that she seems happy in the fog of old age. You even clean out the top drawer of your desk, pausing for a moment to look at the photo of you and your wife in the hospital on the day Apple was born.

"I love that woman," you say to yourself as you're putting on your jacket to go home. "Maybe I'll bring her some flowers."

You walk through the front door of your apartment with a dozen red roses in your hand. Your wife is on the phone with her back to you in the hallway, and—by complete coincidence, it appears—is holding a vase.

You take a few steps toward her and let the door swing closed. When she hears it, she turns toward you.

"I'll have to call you back," she says into the phone, before putting it down softly on the hall table. You notice that her eyes are red.

"What is this?" she asks, holding out the vase.

"It looks like a vase. Perfect place for these roses."

"Who is Diane?" she asks.

Time slows down.

"I have no idea," you reply. "Why?"

"Well, that was Carson Rodriguez's office. They had this delivered here today. You paid for it. And they asked me if I was Diane. So who is Diane?"

"I don't know, honey . . ."

Right then, she launches the vase toward you. You jump out of the way and it smashes into the door and shatters.

"Room three eighteen, you asshole. The Pierre. Are you fucking someone named Diane in the same room where we spent our one-year anniversary? You sick fuck!"

You hear a key in the lock and Apple walks through the door.

"What's with all the glass?" she says, lifting her Candie's clogs as she navigates through piles of broken crystal.

The divorce, ironically, isn't as expensive as the purchases that caused it. You see Apple infrequently, but she does seem to get along with Diane, whom you are now living with in a loft in Tribeca. You're still the CEO of Fleece, although your wife owns half of the shares you used to control, and Sutinis is now the chief financial officer. You make sure all of your personal expenses go through her from now on—you use the crib sheet religiously. After all, you don't want Diane to find out about Tiffany in room 318 at the Pierre.

The end

You and Aaron Rampstein met in 1968 late one night in the textile studios of the Fashion Institute of Technology in New York City. You were trying to finish a mock-up of a hunting sweater that was completely waterproof, and Aaron was building military fatigues that were lightweight but could withstand postnuclear radiation. Both of your projects were due the next morning.

At one point you grew frustrated when you couldn't apply the green dye to the sweater because it was waterproof, and you started cutting up the whole thing.

Aaron came to your aid and said in a very calm voice, "Chill, man. Don't throw the weed out with the bong water. Patience, above all else, is the designer's tool."

He was right. After you both shared a joint, he even offered to help you work on your project. Aaron pointed out that you have to dye the fabric before applying the polymer cross-stitch. Regaining your composure, you worked right till dawn and the sweater looked great. It was raining outside, and Aaron put on the sweater to try it out. Standing in the rain for fifteen minutes, he came back in soaked to the bone everywhere but where the sweater covered him.

You got an A. Aaron got an F for not getting his project in before the semester ended—because he was helping you. Over some beers you both laughed about the grades, and Aaron told you that he couldn't "give a shit" about grades or fashion or anything. "Anyway," he confessed with a mixture of anticipation and dread, "I just got drafted, so I guess the F doesn't matter anyway. I'm going down to Biloxi for basic training next week."

You wrote letters, but after a time he stopped responding. You figured he was too busy getting shot at to write to you. Or, more likely, he'd been killed. You often thought of him as you moved ahead with your life. You worked for the next ten years dividing your time dabbling in the downtown art scene and rubbing elbows with the marketing mavens of Madison Avenue.

You worked your way up the ladder as a competent designer of outdoor wear, all the while keeping the swatch of dyed fabric that Aaron had helped you create that late night in the studio.

In 1982 you founded Fleece Industries—the "Home of the Outdoorsman." In all your early speeches to employees and in any interviews in the smaller fashion trade magazines, you made a point of mentioning Aaron and how fortunate you were to meet him that fateful night, and how sad it was to lose a "friend" and "real American hero" in Vietnam. But as your team of textile engineers worked off the swatch to create the ultimate in protective fashion, getting closer and closer to perfecting its reliability against water, wind, fire, and bullets, the less and less you would mention Aaron's name. Finally, when you broke through with Silk Armor in 1999, you secretly hoped that Aaron had indeed perished in some rice paddy in Asia.

But the dead don't make phone calls. Aaron Rampstein is back, and you know that after all these years, he's not calling to congratulate you.

15 ↑1.75 ADLAC 22 ↓2.60 ENE 50.50 ↑1.50 TYC 60.25 ↓1.75 MSO 65 ↑2

Do you put Aaron out of your mind and return Stubby's call? Whatever Rampstein wants, it can wait another thirty years. Go to page 36.

Or do you return Rampstein's call? After all, you do owe him something for your good fortune. Go to page 156.

The next morning, on the way out of your building, you call Diane and tell her to clear out of the hotel for the day. You head into work and open the vault you had built behind an air vent in your office. You take out one hundred thousand dollars and stuff it into a plastic bag. You make a quick trip over to the Pierre, slip into the room, and leave the bag on the bed before heading back to your office.

You spend the rest of the morning answering e-mails and playing solitaire on your computer. At noon there's a knock at your door. Fawn pokes her head in and says, "Some guy just called and said, 'The package has been delivered.' He hung up before I could ask him what he was talking about."

"That's odd," you say, standing up and reaching for your coat without even realizing it. "Must have been a wrong number. Fawn, I'm going out to meet with some of our bankers for the rest of the afternoon. If anyone calls, tell them I'll get back to them tomorrow morning."

You leave your office as if controlled by an outside force. A tractor beam drawing you to JP's Bar and Grill on Lexington. You enter the old-fashioned bar. The front door slams too hard and you order a scotch—double—before you take a stool.

You've just had a man killed—a man you liked, a man who had a wife and kids. The only way to deal with this is to get blind drunk. You may not go to jail for this, but you will live in hell for the rest of your life.

Six hours later you are still firmly planted at the bar. You have no idea how many drinks you've had. The urge to urinate hits you, and you stumble into the men's room and lean into the first urinal. "He didn't have to die," you mumble to yourself. "He would have kept quiet." You pivot your head and notice a pair of wingtips in the stall. *Did he hear me?* you wonder. You wrestle yourself out of the bathroom and make your way back to your stool. The man with the wingtips exits the bathroom and sits back down where he has been sitting all day: two stools away. He's a stocky redhead with a beer gut that rivals the Buddha. You notice a lump in his jacket. *Is that a gun? A wire?*

You decide he's a cop and it's time to go. You settle up by putting several bills on the bar without even focusing on how much you're leaving. You proceed to walk a drunken serpentine path to the door. On the street you breathe in what is now the chilly night air. Before you've made it to the curb to hail a cab, you hear the door slam behind you. You turn around. Wingtips!

E 15 ↑1.75 ADLAC 22 ↓2.60 ENE 50.50 ↑1.50 TYC 60.25 ↓1.75 MSO 65 ↑2

Do you confront the mystery man with wingtips about his following you? Go to page 58.

Or do you assume that you are just being paranoid and hail a cab to take you home? Go to page 162.

You resist the urge to hug Tiffany, instead putting a fatherly smile on your face. "You know, Tiff, I think that's a great idea. We can hire you at Fleece and get you in front of those cameras. I really don't want to raise any suspicion, though. What kind of office tasks are you good at?"

"I once played a receptionist in a short film," she says chirpily, and then pretends to be answering the phone: "Hello, Fleece Enterprises. How may I direct your call?"

"Fleece Industries, Tiffany, Fleece Industries. Anyway, that won't do—we already have a receptionist."

"Oh! I could be your secretary! That would get me in a ton of shots. Who is that woman who's on the show now? The trashy-looking one with the terrible makeup? Dawn? You should fire her and hire me."

"Her name is Fawn, Tiffany, and she's been with the company for fifteen years. . . . I'm not firing her. She's my right-hand woman."

Tiffany stars pouting, then reaches out and grabs the bulge in your pants. "Are you sure? I'm pretty good with my right hand myself. . . ."

You jump back, nearly falling down before you right yourself against a craft services table.

"Well," says Tiffany, "what do you want me to do, then? I want full benefits, you know."

"I'll find you something," you say. "Just come to the office tomorrow morning around eight and tell Fawn you have an appointment with me."

"Eight A.M.? I'm not even over my jet lag yet!"

"Yes, Tiffany, eight A.M. I'm a busy man. And now I have to go back to work. Another designer to fire." Maybe this wasn't such a great idea after all.

The next day when you arrive at work, you find Fawn and Tiffany sitting ten feet from each other, working hard at pretending the other doesn't exist. Tiffany is holding a cosmetics case open in front of her and applying mascara. Fawn is doing her best to ignore her by filling out expense reports—something she hates to do.

Fawn looks up first. "Good morning, sir. This woman—Brittany, is it?"

"Tiffany." Cold as ice.

"Tiffany, of course, excuse me. She says she has an appointment with you, but I don't have it anywhere on your schedule."

You look over at Tiffany. She's glaring at Fawn with a look like she wants to rip her head off and stuff it down her throat. You turn back to Fawn. She's got a querulous look on her face.

"Ah, yes, yes," you say, trying to sound as if you'd forgotten to tell Fawn about the meeting with Tiffany. "Fawn . . . this is Tiffany, a friend of Stu Kovacs's from Los Angeles. . . . Find a position for her. Helping out Stu is good for all of us."

"There's nowhere to put her. We don't have any openings."

"Well, I could always use a second assistant," you say, knowing it will infuriate Fawn.

Fawn is visibly rattled but then appears to have an epiphany. "Well, Josh the intern has gone back to school, and we need someone to help out in the mail room," she says, wearing her best catfight grin.

Tiffany stands up. "Mail room? Do you really think I'll work in a mail room?"

"If Fawn says that's the only job we have open, I'm afraid it's the only job we have open." Tiffany looks like she's about to explode. Fawn stifles a giggle, and Tiffany takes a step toward her.

Just then the elevator doors open and the camera crew walks out. Seeing you, the cameraman quickly starts walking toward you. The red light on the camera switches on. When he's reached you, he turns the camera toward Tiffany, who has transformed into a smiling, dovelike presence.

"Where can I find the mailroom?" she asks, only looking at

Fawn briefly before turning back toward the camera. She looks like the D-list actress that she is.

"It's right down the hall, this way," says Fawn, standing up. "Let me show you where we keep the smocks. . . ."

↑ 1.75 ADLAC 22 ↓ 2.60 ENE 50.50 ↑ 1.50 TYC 60.25 ↓ 1.75 MSO 65 ↑ 2.50

Go to page 210.

You take a breath and dial the number—it's a New York area code. You're hoping the call will go to voice mail, but it only rings once before he picks up.

"Hey, old friend. How are you? I saw your face on the television this morning and wanted to call and congratulate you. It's been so long."

It's definitely Rampstein—he's still got the remarkably calm voice he had as a youth. You can't quite believe what you're hearing.

"God, I thought you were dead. I never heard from you. How are you? Are you married? Where have you been?" You rattle off the questions in quick succession with nervous energy.

"I'm good, I'm good. Let's get together and celebrate your success. What do you say to a drink tonight?" So calm. He's getting to something.

"Oh, I can't tonight. Spending time with the family and some friends."

"I'm a friend, right? I helped you create Silk Armor. Isn't that a friendly thing to do?"

"Well, you didn't help me create Silk Armor, I developed it over many years. You just showed me how to dye the fabric."

"Life would've been different for me if I hadn't helped you get an A that night and failed the class myself as a result."

"Rampstein, calm down," you say. "Listen, I can give you some money if that's what you need."

"Some money? I want a lot of money, you piece of shit. A lot of money."

"Where are you staying?" you ask him.

"Hell's Angels headquarters on East Third Street."

"Hell's Angels? You're in the Hell's Angels?"

"No. I just designed their new logo, so they're letting me bunk down here while I'm in town. But don't you worry about that. I'll be in touch. Looking forward to that drink tonight." And he hangs up.

What *should* be the day that you've always dreamed about becomes the nightmare that you've always feared.

You lose yourself in worst-case scenarios as you stare into the picture of you, your wife, and your daughter waving from a canoe at your Maine lake house, when Fawn pops her head in.

"The camera crew from CNN is here for your interview."

Go to page 179.

You tell Carson that Fleece will be paying for everything, and then ask him if he can come back Monday. "I've had a long week," you say by way of explanation. But you really just want him out of there.

You wake up the next morning, thankful that it's a Saturday. Maybe you'll head down to the NYAC to play a couple of games of squash and then head on up to the boat basin for a burger and beer.

Your wife comes out of the bathroom, already dressed, with her makeup on. "Honey, you're going to need to stay home today. Carson ordered a bunch of stuff that will be delivered in several batches. Apple and I are having a ladies day. We're going to Bliss for spa treatments and then shoe shopping at Prada. We'll be back for dinner."

"Isn't there anyone else who can take care of this? I'm the CEO of a public company, for God's sake."

"But I'm the CEO of this house, and today you're doing your part." Before you can protest, she's out the bedroom door and clickety-clacking down the stairs.

The shipments start arriving by 10:00 A.M.

The first thing the moving men unwrap is some sort of umbrella stand. It's shaped like an Egyptian monkey holding what looks to be a papaya—or its own dung.

"Where should I put this?" asks the mover, barely containing his laughter.

"Just leave it there," you say, embarrassed by the absurdity of the thing.

It gets worse. A courier arrives with a platinum-plated wastebasket. FedEx brings something that looks like a pincushion. The parade is endless: sheets, coat hangers, an appointment book, a sewing basket, and a traveling toilette box. The last to arrive are two impeccably dressed Indian men carrying a pole with a shower curtain hanging on it.

You sign for it and tell them to put it on the couch.

"No, sir, we cannot. The curtain can never be folded. We must hang it before we leave." The stoicism on this little man's face tells you that you would be fighting a losing battle were you to protest. This is one serious shower curtain. You direct them to the bathroom. As they march down the hall, you look down at the invoice to see how much a holy shower curtain costs.

Carson Rodriguez

Design for Home and Office

T o k y o • M i l a n • C a i r o • N e w Y o r k

By Appointment Only!

Monsoon Shower Curtain: $6,000
Ruby Inlay Toilette Box: $17,000
Kenya Universe Umbrella Stand: $15,000
Hearth and Strong Sewing Basket: $6,300
Sempre Dormo Bedsheets: $5,900
M. Dearest Coat Hangers: $2,900
Circular File Wastebasket: $2,200
Sharpest Image Appointment Book: $1,650
Emperor's Pincushion: $445

Total owed to Carson: $57,395

Pay promptly, please!

Go to page 217.

You turn off the television. Your wife jumps off the bed so fast that she knocks your elbow and spills the scalding hot coffee all over your bare thighs.

She has no sympathy for you right now. "You liar! The last two days were the best days we've had in years, and you were lying to me!"

"I haven't! I'm fucking burnt!" You are soaking up the coffee with a pillow and your legs are pulsing with pain.

"You lied to me at the one moment in your miserable life that you should have told the truth!"

You did lie to her.

"I swear to God! Honey, I don't know what the fuck is going on! But I'm going to get to the bottom of this."

You just lied to her again.

You continue, "I can't believe you think I would be a part of a corrupt plot. I thought we had rebuilt something here."

And you made her feel guilty.

Go to page 238.

"As tempting as it is to put all of this on the company's tab, I think I'd have a tough time putting in a receipt for a ten-thousand-dollar kitchen boulder," you say as you walk between your wife and Carson to get yourself a pilsner out of the fridge. "Anyway, if the invoices come to me, I can have some aesthetic control over what goes on in my own home. That's fair, right?"

Your wife has crossed her arms and is looking at you like she has many, many times before—on occasions when you've been rude to waiters, curt to cab drivers, and hard on Apple. You look at her and roll your eyes as you pop open your ice-cold beer.

"I just hope, for your sake, that my artistic capabilities are not compromised by stinginess," says Carson. "I understand that you don't want to let go of the old fraternity years. Should I hang some old license plates on the wall? Perhaps a neon 'Schlitz Beer' sign? I must have complete control over my vision or I walk!" As he finishes his tirade, Carson holds a sprig of saffron close to his nose and gives you the stare down.

"You will not be compromised, and my husband will behave himself. He may be the boss at work, but I run the show in here." Your wife looks right at you the whole time she is speaking. She then puts her arm around Carson and says, "Why don't you show me where you think the bidet should go." This brightens him up, and he takes her hand and practically skips out of the room.

5 ↑ 1.75 ADLAC 22 ↓ 2.60 ENE 50.50 ↑ 1.50 TYC 60.25 ↓ 1.75 MSO 65 ↑ 2.58

Go to page 47.

You stare at Wingtips for another second or two and then turn away. He also starts walking away. Whew, thank God you didn't do something stupid. You've got to be careful not to do anything out of the ordinary for the next few days . . . like drinking yourself into a stupor. You're a fool! You've got to get home and get everything back to normal, or at least create the appearance of normal.

You arrive home twenty minutes later to find an empty apartment. *Where the hell are they?* you wonder. *It must be two in the morning.* You look up at the clock on the wall—it's only 8:30 P.M. You realize yet again how drunk you are and decide that the best strategy would be to go directly to bed.

You wake up at 5:45 A.M. with the worst headache you've had in years. You rush downstairs to grab the paper from your front door. Quickly scanning it, you see that there's no word of Weiss's death. You wonder what St. James did with the body.

You go back upstairs, tiptoe by the bed into the bathroom so as not to wake your wife, and take a long hot shower. You would like nothing better than to work from home today, but you know you have to keep up appearances. After dressing, though, you can't even make it to the door of your bedroom before you feel nauseous. You lie down beside your still-sleeping wife. She opens her eyes and looks at you.

"Honey, you're up early. You were knocked out when we got home last night. You must be exhausted."

"I am. But I really have to get to work. I have a lot of stuff to talk to Weiss about to get our accounting department ready to handle the increased workload of being public."

"Weiss? I haven't seen him or his sweet wife in a while. Why don't we have them over to dinner sometime soon? Didn't he just have his second child? A boy? Did we send them a gift?"

You can't take this. "Sweetie, I don't remember. But I have to go." You kiss her on the forehead and tuck the sheets up around her shoulders. "Go back to sleep."

You head down to your waiting car.

You're in your office by 6:30 A.M. and you are the only one there. You go into Weiss's office and look for clues to determine if he had plans to sell you out. You look through his drawers and browse through his e-mail. You hope that in all of his mania, he didn't do something stupid like write a confession letter. You do find a picture taped to his monitor. It's a snapshot of Weiss in operating room scrubs, smiling and holding his new son, Jack.

"Sorry, Jack," you say to the photo. "But don't worry, you'll be well taken care of."

You exit Weiss's office, and standing right in front of you is Ms. Sutinis.

"Hi, Ms. Sutinis. You're in early."

"Good morning. You're in early yourself. Don't worry about Weiss. There's nothing in there. I checked. You're in good hands with me." She starts to walk away, then stops after a few paces and looks at you. She opens her mouth as if to say something, but then closes it again, turns, and walks away whistling Wagner's "Ride of the Valkyries."

You go to your office and lie down on the couch, not knowing if the terrible knot in your stomach is guilt or just a vicious hangover. Before you can figure it out, you've dozed off. Fawn wakes you up when she comes into your office two hours later.

"Sorry to wake you, but Phyllis just called. Larry didn't come home last night. She's terribly upset. Can you talk to her?"

"Sure. Of course. I don't know where he is, but I'll talk to her."

Fawn scurries to the door and opens it to find Ms. Sutinis standing there.

"I was just coming to talk to you about our fourth-quarter projections," says Sutinis. "We need to make a statement to the Street."

You sense an opportunity to show concern about Weiss's disappearance in front of Fawn. "Ms. Sutinis, you haven't seen Larry Weiss around, have you?"

"Well," she begins, looking right into your eyes, "shortly after our meeting yesterday morning, I went to Starbucks to get a coffee. On the way back, I saw Weiss get into a cab with a tall brunette woman. He had a suitcase with him. I just assumed she was his wife. Mrs. Weiss isn't a model, is she?"

Fawn gasps. "No—she's a lab technician. Oh my God! Weiss ran away with another woman!"

"Put Phyllis through," you snap at Fawn. "She needs a friend right now!"

Fawn blows past Sutinis, whose gaze has never left your eyes. She cocks her head, smiles, and leaves.

The phone rings and you pick it up to comfort an old friend who has just lost her husband . . . to another woman.

Go to page 224.

You've been getting lots of press about your show. You are on the cover of not only every business magazine, but also every entertainment rag in America. *Us Weekly* labeled you as a reality star "cut from a different cloth." *Entertainment Weekly* writes that you're the man who "brought the CEO back into fashion." And *People* has touted you as the "Sexiest Man Alive"—you took the title from Jude Law.

The whole show is shot in your office and home, except the scenes where you let people go. These are shot on a soundstage in Queens that's made up to look like a fashion show. The designers have models strut their fashions on the catwalk, and then you decide who stays and who goes right there on the spot.

One day while at the studio in Queens, shortly after you've been informed that you've topped the Nielsen ratings, you decide to go outside and grab a breath of fresh air during a break in shooting. (Of course, there's a camera crew following you for separate footage. They're always following you.) As you approach the front door, you notice a tall blond woman screaming at the security guard from the other side of the turnstiles.

"I am a personal friend of the star!" she yells.

"Yeah, yeah. So am I. So is everybody," he says in response, not budging an inch.

Just then she looks up at you. You think you recognize her, but then again, you've given so many autographs these days, it's hard to keep track of all the beautiful women.

"There he is," she says. "He'll tell you."

It's Tiffany.

5 ↑ 1.75 ADLAC 22 ↓ 2.60 ENE 50.50 ↑ 1.50 TYC 60.25 ↓ 1.75 MSO 65 ↑ 2.50

Go to page 228.

"It's Dan the doorman," you hear as you put the phone to your ear. "The entire building is on fire—and the firemen are saying it looks like it started in your apartment!"

You pay your bill and get a cab home, just in time to see the fire engine ladder being retracted and a fireman shaking his head in amazement at the smoldering heap that used to be your home.

The cause of the fire seemed to be a lit joint in Apple's desk. (She did seem a little distracted earlier. She didn't laugh at your joke, she ordered her meal twice, and she ate a lot more than she usually does.)

You have homeowner's insurance, of course, but you hadn't yet managed to include any of the purchases you'd made with Carson. So while the fire wasn't a complete loss, you find your-self almost a million dollars short once you've done a quick reckoning of your accounts.

You and your wife send Apple off to rehab at Seven Hills and then proceed to separate and ultimately get divorced. The fire made you realize that the two of you were never that com-patible after all. You resign your post as CEO of Fleece, taking only the title of chief textile engineer, and dedicate yourself to that which always made you happy: not the money, not the business, but your love of innovation and the eternal search for better clothing.

The end

When you get back to the office, everything is in chaos. Investigators have made a pile of computers in the corner of the lobby, and a hard-looking man with a pistol in his belt is guarding the stack.

"Where is Barry?" you say to the first employee you see.

"He's in your office, sir, talking to the Securities and Exchange Commission."

You walk into your office. Barry is arguing strenuously with someone, and he seems relieved when he sees you. He flicks his eyes toward your desk and back to indicate the missing computer.

You ask the investigators for a few minutes with your corporate counsel, and the two of you squeeze into your bathroom.

"They're not going to find it unless they use a Trident submarine," you tell Barry.

"Did you sell shares of Fleece the day before we announced the T-shirt failures?" he asks with a look of incredulity. "They say they have the trade tickets from TownGroup and that it's the most clear-cut case of insider trading they've ever seen."

You look at Barry. This man is one of your oldest friends and he knows you're lying to him. And you will continue to do so.

"I might have. . . . I can't recall. But I didn't hear about the T-shirt failures until Friday morning, so how could I be guilty of insider trading?"

"What are you talking about? Remember I came and told you on Thursday about the phone call from the clerk at the Joint Chiefs? It seems that right after I left your office, you called Felix and told him to sell your shares, which you didn't tell me, by the way. And then you said we should wait until after the government's announcement to respond. I was never quite sure why, but it makes a whole lot of sense now."

The bastard, you think. *He must be wearing a wire.*

"I have no idea what you're talking about, Barry," you say, as the corners of your mouth turn up in a small smile.

5 ↑1.75 ADLAC 22 ↓2.60 ENE 50.50 ↑1.50 TYC 60.25 ↓1.75 MSO 65 ↑2.5

Go to page 170.

"Do what you have to do, Baldacker. Do what you have to do."

Baldacker nods and leaves your office. You pick up the phone and call your wife.

"Honey, let's go out to dinner tonight. Remember I was telling you about how badly we'd done this quarter? It turns out there was a spike in sales in Asia the last couple of weeks, and we're coming out just about where we expected in the first place."

"Oh, sweetie. That's wonderful. I told you that you'd be rewarded for turning down the government contract."

"Well, you were right. I guess doing the right thing is always the best choice," you say, with a twinge of guilt about the fact that you're lying to your wife while she's praising your morality.

"So where do you want to go?" she asks.

"You pick," you say, suddenly wanting off the phone. "I'll be out of here around six. Make reservations for seven o'clock. And let's not bring Apple. I want this to be a 'date night' for us."

The rest of the day passes without incident. You find yourself going back to the piece of paper Baldacker gave you and staring at the numbers he'd put together. *This better work*, you think as you stuff the paper into your briefcase at five minutes to six. You tell Fawn you're going home for the evening and head out onto Madison Avenue.

Your wife chose her favorite restaurant, Chez Brigitte, a narrow countertop French restaurant run like an American coffee shop. It was the first restaurant you both ate at when you moved to New York City, because it was next door to your tiny West Village apartment.

You arrive on Greenwich Avenue, outside Chez Brigitte. You step out of the car and see your wife dashing inside to get out of the sprinkling rain. You both go in and squeeze yourselves onto the last stools by the window. Your face is sweating like the condensation beading on the restaurant's window.

"You look haggard," she says, rubbing your back as you get settled on your stool.

"It's been a rough couple of weeks. I'm just so glad that we're going to come out okay. And we are. We'll never move backward, my dear. I promised you that when I proposed. Do you believe in me?"

"I love you," she says, because she truly does.

At this moment you realize two things: You just got away with the most sincere sounding lie you've ever told, and the waitress has fantastic tits.

Go to page 172.

The government's pursuit of you turns into a two-year media circus. It takes them eighteen months to press charges, and since they can't find enough hard evidence to actually charge you with insider trading, they charge you with obstruction of justice based on the IT guy's testimony that you tried to delete your meeting with Barry. You begin the torture of a public trial.

Each morning you have to make your way through the phalanx of photographers camped on the courthouse steps. In a kind gesture, Attorney General Craven Albanie has let you and your team use a "war room" on the fourth floor of the courthouse to plot your defense. You eat a catered lunch in private, and have Fawn—who is sticking with you to the end—bring bottles of Evian and bottled green tea from Japan to drink at the defense table during the trial.

You were right about Barry. He *was* wearing a wire when he so blatantly tried to get you to admit to insider trading. Your revenge was to fire him before the trial started. Your board has decided to back you until you're found guilty.

Still, the trial itself is a complete embarrassment.

Fawn breaks down crying on the stand, saying, "He cares so much."

The parents of Pat Mayhew take the stand to say that they never received a word of contrition from you, either in person or in a letter.

When Felix takes the stand, you start to feel the trial slipping away from you. "I have never, ever been treated so rudely on the telephone," he says.

The jury returns with bad news: You have been found guilty of obstruction. You're going to jail.

15 ↑1.75 ADLAC 22 ↓2.60 ENE 50.50 ↑1.50 TYC 60.25 ↓1.75 MSO 65 ↑2.

Go to page 204.

It's almost noon when you decide to call Stu on your cell phone from the smoothie bar at the Reebok café. It seems like as good a place as any to make a TV deal. You dial his number.

"Stu Kovacs's office."

"Hi, is Stu in?"

"Who, may I ask, is calling?"

"Tell him it's the idiot clothing designer he kicked out of his office two days ago."

"Okay, please hold."

You wait for several minutes before Kovacs comes on the line.

"What?"

"Mr. Kovacs, it's me, the CEO of Fleece."

"I know who it is. The time-robber from the east. Make it fast."

"Well, I was thinking about what you said about branding myself, and I think it would be a great idea to put together a reality TV show . . ."

Just like last time, the conversation turns one-sided.

" . . . about your life. Perfect. Great idea. I love it. I'll produce it, and you'll listen to every word I say. We'll shoot you every day, all day. At home and in the office. We'll get you to hire some designers on a trial basis and you can fire them one by one until you're left with one designer at the end of the show. I'll draft up some contracts and send them to your office. We'll start off with a one-year contract. That's all I'm willing to give you. And before I hang up, I have to tell you to lose weight. You look like a Danish stuffed into spandex."

"What about a name?" you say. "I was thinking *The Simple Stitch*."

"Fine," he says. "I don't give a damn. I'll make it a hit whatever stupid name you want to give it."

He hangs up. You don't know if the feeling in your stomach is the result of embarrassment or excitement, but you're about to be a TV star.

.5 ↑ 1.75 ADLAC 22 ↓ 2.60 ENE 50.50 ↑ 1.50 TYC 60.25 ↓ 1.75 MSO 65 ↑ 2.5

Go to page 203.

The next morning you're lying in bed with your wife at 9:30. You decided around 3:30 in the morning—after your third round of making love—that you were going to go in to the office late, despite the fact that you have your quarterly analyst meeting this afternoon at the St. Regis Hotel.

"Honey, can we go on a vacation soon?" she asks. "You've been working so hard, and I think you need a rest."

"No rest for the wicked, my dear," you say as you pop out of bed. "We were wicked last night, weren't we? What was that position again? The napping frog?"

She laughs as you walk into the bathroom and shut the door behind you.

An hour later you greet Fawn with a cheery, "Good morning, sweetheart. Has Baldacker been by? I need the final quarterly results to look over before our meeting this afternoon."

"Yes, he left this package for you," she says.

You spend the next two hours rehearsing your speech for this afternoon and then head over to the St. Regis.

Just before the meeting starts, you're sitting at the bar of the hotel sipping a glass of Johnnie Walker Blue. You wouldn't normally be sneaking in a drink in the middle of the day, but this is not a normal day. You are about to go upstairs to a conference room and do an acting job that no actor would envy, especially when the audience is filled with Wall Streeters who have a terrific nose for blood. You gulp back the last of the scotch, push yourself away from the bar, and head into the hotel lobby, walking like Gregory Peck in his role as Atticus Finch in *To Kill a Mockingbird*.

Within two minutes of your speech to the analysts, they are no longer listening to you. All they needed to hear from you was "just shy of projections, but very strong," and everybody had their heads down punching away at their BlackBerrys or ducking out the door to call their firms' brokers and tell them to buy, buy, buy! Before you have even finished your report, the good news is already front-page news on every financial Web site. Wall Street's so-called "whisper number" had your earnings falling by 50 percent, so investors are jubilant.

5 ↑ 1.75 ADLAC 22 ↓ 2.60 ENE 50.50 ↑ 1.50 TYC 60.25 ↓ 1.75 MSO 65 ↑ 2.50

Go to page 231.

The MSNBC interview goes swimmingly, as does your *Today* show pretaped interview with Hal Roebler, the jolly Santa-like weatherman. The two of you put on Silk Armor trench coats and enter Fleece's hi-tech "wet room," where you are sprayed with water hoses and come out dry as a bone. You also wish happy birthday to Rose Gumpler, who will turn 108 tomorrow, and promise to send her a Silk Armor shawl to protect against spilled tea.

Fleece stock ends the day up ten percent from the opening bell. The word on Wall Street is that there was "enthusiastic" trading of the stock, that Fleece is the kind of investment that comes around only every century or so. The company's products are hi-tech but practical, making it an investment that energizes both short-term traders and long-term investors. The "Money Bunny" labels the stock as having "long-term growth and short-term pizzazz."

Whatever that means, you think as you watch the closing bell stock roundup in your car, heading north to your duplex apartment on Riverside and Ninety-fifth Street. It's been a good day overall. You hope Rampstein will ask for a payoff and then just leave you alone.

You arrive at your building and your doorman opens the car door. "Good evening, sir."

"Good evening, Don."

"Dan."

"Right. Have a good evening," you say as Dan runs ahead of you to open the building door. You enter the elevator, and as the doors close, you notice Dan picking up the house phone and dialing.

You open your apartment door and your home is strangely dark. Immediately your imagination goes equally dark. *Rampstein is in here with some of his biker buddies. They've tied up my wife and daughter and are going to make me watch them kill my family!*

"Honey, I'm home. Honey, are you here?" You flick the light switch by the door and are startled by shouts of "Surprise!"

It's everyone you know, and they all look ridiculous with party hats on their heads and horns in their mouths. You even spot a sheep-shaped piñata hanging from your living room chandelier.

Your wife runs up to you with two glasses of champagne. She kisses you full on the mouth and hands you a glass. "To the man who indeed captured the Golden Fleece! We love you!"

"Hip hip hooray!" yells the crowd of friends and family, with smiles from ear to ear. Just then you feel a vibration in your pocket. It's your BlackBerry. You take it out to shut it off and notice a text message that simply reads CHK YR EMAIL.

You have no doubt who sent it.

5 ↑ 1.75 ADLAC 22 ↓ 2.60 ENE 50.50 ↑ 1.50 TYC 60.25 ↓ 1.75 MSO 65 ↑ 2.5E

Go to page 178.

You call your IT department and have them send a guy over.

A blond skate rat wearing an anime shirt, black jeans, and white sneakers lopes into your office.

"I somehow deleted something on my calendar by mistake and I need to get it back," you explain.

He looks at your screen. "Where? Here? But that was last week. Does it really matter now? It's not like you're going to miss any appointments or anything."

"My memoirs. It's for my memoirs. I have to keep a meticulous record so I know what I did, hour by hour and day by day."

"Memoirs, huh? Can't wait for the movie." He's looking at you, despite his best efforts to hide his true feelings, like he just can't believe how arrogant you are.

"Just see if you can get it back, will you?"

He sits down at your desk, makes a few mouse clicks, and then stands up. "There. I'm sure your meeting with Barry will make for a real page-turner of a chapter in your 'memoirs.'"

As a special bonus for you, he programs a scroll bar on your desktop that gives you up-to-the-minute stock prices. He then leaves your office without closing the door, leaving you to get up and close it.

You sit down at your desk and try to figure out the odds of your being caught.

First of all, no one really watches that windbag on CNN anymore, and if someone in a position to be curious about the Thursday/Friday discrepancy was watching it, you doubt they would have caught Barry's slip. And even if they did, maybe they wouldn't have the wherewithal to look at your calendar and put the chronology of your meeting with Barry and the share sale in place. *What was I so worried about?* you wonder.

15 ↑1.75 ADLAC 22 ↓2.60 ENE 50.50 ↑1.50 TYC 60.25 ↓1.75 MSO 65 ↑2.

Go to page 181.

Less than a week later you're standing on the field of Swamplands Stadium watching your first practice as the owner of a football team. They're no longer called the Corporals; they're now the Argonauts. Araz and Jeff are furiously putting together a new uniform that has an ancient Greek ship with a ram on the deck sporting a coat of golden fleece.

You're pacing the sideline with Red Simpson, the head coach, watching the players—all of whom seem absurdly large when you get this close to them—running wind sprints and the like. The day is, for the most part, a blast, even if most of the good times come at your expense. The quarterback, Lance Fallow, throws you a ball and it bounces right off your chest. Trying to kick a field goal, you kick the tee right out from under the football, leaving the ball on the ground exactly where it was placed. Picking it up, you try to make a pass to the running back who was waiting for your kick, and it only makes it about halfway, hitting Simpson in the back of the head. "He throws like a girl," you hear one of the linemen say.

But you're a good sport about it, making jokes about keeping your day job. The day's highlight: Three members of the team sneak up behind you and pour a bucket of Gatorade over your head.

↑ 1.75 ADLAC 22 ↓ 2.60 ENE 50.50 ↑ 1.50 TYC 60.25 ↓ 1.75 MSO 65 ↑ 2.50

Go to page 218.

You excuse yourself from the party despite your wife's protests and slip into your den. You take a deep breath and open up your laptop to read your e-mail in private. You see one new message with no subject, from *YouOweMe@EatLead.com*. You look over your shoulder to make sure the coast is clear, and then you open the e-mail. You read the one line: "Meet me at the Hell's Angels headquarters at 9:30 P.M. or I will come after you."

You delete the e-mail and empty the trash folder. You look at your watch; it's 8:45. You have forty-five minutes to get to the East Village. But first you have to leave your own party. You get up from your chair, and your knees feel like pudding. You walk into the living room and immediately bump into a waiter, knocking over his silver tray of mini crab cakes. The crash of the tray hitting the floor gets everyone's attention.

"Sorry, everyone. But I have to step out for about an hour. A CEO's work is never done!" You should win an Oscar for the acting job you're delivering. Your wife approaches you, visibly annoyed.

"Honey, can't whatever this is wait until tomorrow?" she asks, squeezing your arm.

"I'm sorry. The Tokyo market opens in forty-five minutes and the CEO of the exchange wants to have a quick conference call before Fleece stock debuts. And I have none of my notes here. I'm sorry. I'll be back in time for dinner."

You kiss your wife on the cheek and leave your apartment in the same anxious silence that you found it in only five minutes earlier. You hop into a cab, and within twenty-five minutes you are knocking on the door of the Hell's Angels headquarters. You are scared out of your mind.

The door opens. A huge, fat biker is standing there with a pool cue in his hand. He just stands there, blocking the entrance and eyeing your suit.

"I'm here to see Aaron Rampstein. Is he around?"

"Oh yeah, you're the millionaire," says the fat biker. "We've been waiting for you. Come on in."

E 15 ↑1.75 ADLAC 22 ↓2.60 ENE 50.50 ↑1.50 TYC 60.25 ↓1.75 MSO 65 ↑2

Go to page 245.

"Ah, yes, Fawn . . . tell them I'll be there in a minute."

She pulls the door closed. You realize that you've suddenly soaked right through your shirt. You can't go on TV with sweat stains everywhere! You frantically look around your office for something to wear. There's only one thing: a pink, extra-large Fleece fleece, which you had planned to send over to Rosie O' Donnell to see if she would wear it on her show.

With no other options, you quickly strip off your shirt and tie and pull on the pink fleece. You wipe the sweat from your forehead, spit on your comb and run it through your salt-and-pepper hair, then head out to face the cameras. When you open your door, you see about a half-dozen people sitting on the ground amid piles of equipment. Somebody starts giggling.

"Thank you for coming by today," you say. "How about a tour?"

The CNN reporter, Martha Blalock, is a striking woman with short blond hair who used to act in one of those cop shows before becoming a journalist. It calms you down to give her the tour and do a little flirting. "These are our main offices where all the big decisions are made. We do have a clothing test center, which we call 'The Lab'—that's where all the testing of the new innovations in our clothing takes place. It's a lot like the James Bond movies; we blow up sweaters, soak running shoes in battery acid, and submit our ski parkas to temperatures only found on the planet Pluto. We even have an Iranian centrifuge. It's very cool."

The piece goes remarkably smoothly, except for when Martha asks you how you invented the technology behind Silk Armor. At that moment you start thinking that Rampstein might even be in the building, and you can't focus on the camera anymore. After a few moments of complete panic, however, you recover and give her your standard response about an Indian shaman in New Mexico. You even manage to squeeze in a few jokes about the pink fleece that you're wearing. All the while, though, you can't stop thinking about Rampstein.

The crew leaves wearing the Fleece pullovers that you had Fawn get for them. Dealing with media people is the easiest thing. Throw them a free lunch and some swag, and they'll paint the prettiest picture of you.

You go into your office and fall on the couch, putting a throw pillow over your face to try and hide from the world while you wait for your next call from Rampstein.

Fawn pops her head into your office. "Sorry to bother you, but a camera crew from MSNBC is here."

E 15 ↑1.75 ADLAC 22 ↓2.60 ENE 50.50 ↑1.50 TYC 60.25 ↓1.75 MSO 65 ↑2

Go to page 174.

Despite your calculations of the odds of getting caught, you start taking your laptop home from the office every day, just in case. You think about all the idiots who have gotten busted for financial crimes through records of their e-mails. You're not going to make it easy for anyone to take you down.

You also begin to treat Fawn much better than you have of late. You'll need her to get your back if the shit goes down. You suggest that the two of you rent a boat from Chelsea Piers and go out for a cruise around Manhattan. She readily agrees.

The two of you are reclining in the back of the boat out on the Hudson River, sipping Amstel Lights, when your cell phone rings. It's Barry.

"Boss, the SEC is in the office, impounding computers. They're saying something about insider trading. You've got to get back here."

You look down at your briefcase, which luckily contains your laptop. "I'll be there as soon as I can, Barry," you say, slamming your phone shut. You tell Fawn you've got to get back to the city, and ask her to take the wheel of the boat. When she's not looking, you lean down, open your briefcase, pull out your laptop, and throw it into the Hudson.

Good luck finding that, you think.

↑ 1.75 ADLAC 22 ↓ 2.60 ENE 50.50 ↑ 1.50 TYC 60.25 ↓ 1.75 MSO 65 ↑ 2.50

Go to page 167.

The next thirty-six hours shake the foundation of your marriage to its core. Sally Laufetter is exactly the kind of woman you have always wanted—sexy and smart, the kind of woman who is capable of dressing to the nines or smoking cigars with the boys at the club. She's twenty years younger than you, and while your wife is getting a little saggy around the edges, Laufetter tells you you're the most physically fit CEO she's ever come across. The two of you can't keep your eyes—or your hands—off each other. And it feels *meaningful*.

She's also extremely forward. "I think you should leave your wife. Today. When you get home. I have to get rid of a little boy toy I have living in my basement, but that's been a purely physical relationship. With you I've found the union of mind and body, business and pleasure. And I don't want to let you get away."

"But Sally," you say, "as I told you, Fleece has invested millions in a new campaign that revolves around my image. My image as a devoted husband and father, and as a focused CEO. It could all come crumbling down. And then what would we have?"

"Harry isn't about being squeaky clean," she replies. "Harry is about being your own man. Making your own moves. You might do something that people may not agree with, but they sure have to respect you. It's exactly how you've built your whole career. Don't you see that?"

`15 ↑1.75 ADLAC 22 ↓2.60 ENE 50.50 ↑1.50 TYC 60.25 ↓1.75 MSO 65 ↑2.`

Do you see it? Maybe it is time for a new start. Go to page 44.
Or do you not see it? Do you instead see the downside to such a move and decide to protect your marriage and, more important, your brand? Go to page 56.

"You're right, Baldacker. Spell out the loan as clearly as you think is appropriate in the quarterly filing. I can handle the board. I don't think our investors are going to have a problem with it anyway, considering the boost in Fleece merchandise sales this team has already given us."

He gives you a look you interpret as something akin to admiration, gathers his papers, and leaves your office.

And it turns out you were right. Investors don't even pay attention to Fleece's exposure to your loan, and the board is behind you 100 percent of the way. "Hell, man, we want you to buy more sports teams," says Clark Henderson, the most ball-busting member of the board, "if you can get a boost like this in Fleece sales by doing so. Christ, it's the first smart thing you've done in quite some time. . . ."

You let his backhanded compliment slide, thinking instead of your travel arrangements to Seattle next weekend. It may sound corny to some, but you plan to hike up Mt. Olympus with Apple when you're out there. You want to try out the new insect-repellant Fleece line, Don't Bug Me.

↑ 1.75 ADLAC 22 ↓ 2.60 ENE 50.50 ↑ 1.50 TYC 60.25 ↓ 1.75 MSO 65 ↑ 2.50

Go to page 41

You follow Kovacs into his office, which is styled like a bungalow. Open windows and wicker couches and posters of every movie that you've heard of but never bothered to see. You sit in a wicker chair across from Stu, who sits at his desk, sucking back the last of his beet shake. He then tosses the empty cup in the bamboo trash can without looking, as if to signify the start of his speech.

"Listen. I know why you're here, so save the spiel. I also know that I'm the last person you've talked to in town, so be aware that I think you're an asshole. That being said, I think you're an idiot for doing what you want to do. Putting your clothes on movie stars is not going to give you the revenue bump that you think. With ideas like yours, I'm surprised your stock hasn't started trading for rubles. Do me a favor—do yourself a favor—and don't think of any more ideas. Do you want to sell clothes? I mean a lot of clothes?"

You don't bother to answer his question, as you know he doesn't care about what you have to say. At this point Stu is springing up and down in his chair like a baby in a high chair.

"I'm going to give you some advice, if only to get you out of my office sooner rather than later. If you want to sell a brand, you have to put a face on the brand. Not someone else's face either. People want to know what they're buying before they buy it. You want the people to buy you. You want them to buy into your idea of what it is to be outdoors, buy into your idea of what it means to be fashionable, buy into your idea of what it means to wear Silk Armor. I'll tell you something right now. The girl I'm banging wears Silk Armor pajamas! She loves the way they feel. But imagine if she were thinking about your face every time she slipped her bare ass into one of your pajama pants. If you want to sell clothes, do two things: Never come back to Hollywood again, and put your face on the product you're selling." He pauses, clearly finished with his monologue, and adds, "Don't let the door hit you on the ass on your way out."

Stu then picks up the phone and speed-dials a number. "Georgia, the rushes on *Forever Tomorrow* are brilliant! . . . Yeah, I was watching them at home. The redheaded boy burying his dead golden retriever was genius!"

You stand up from the chair, walk out of his office, and close the door. You pass by Stu's secretary, who is now doing the *TV Guide* crossword, and you walk back out onto the lot. The California sun is bright. You don't know whether you should throw a rock through Stu's window or take his advice and brand yourself.

↑ 1.75 ADLAC 22 ↓ 2.60 ENE 50.50 ↑ 1.50 TYC 60.25 ↓ 1.75 MSO 65 ↑ 2.50

Despite the torture this little bastard inflicted on your ego, do you take Stu's advice and brand yourself to sell Fleece clothing? Go to page 85.

Or do you pick up a smooth stone from the faux Zen rock garden on the lot and throw it through Stu's window? Go to page 72.

You sit in your office for several minutes, unable to think clearly. How on Earth are you going to have Weiss killed? You don't know any hit men. You don't really even know any violent men. Except perhaps Weiss, in his current state of mind.

Then it hits you. Way back when, you developed a line of Fleece's bulletproof outdoor gear for an Idaho hunting club. You'd thought they were just gun enthusiasts at the time, but they turned out to be a militia that was recruiting and training under-age kids for a small army assault on the offices of the Internal Revenue Service. There was a huge bust, and most of them had gone to jail. They'd even made a *Law & Order* episode based on the story. You could try and track down the leader. If he's not up for the job, surely he'll know some crazy who would be.

You hit your intercom. "Fawn, remember that group, DONUT—Defenders Of the NU Tomorrow? Do we still have contact information for that guy, what was his name? John St. James?"

"Um, I think we do," she says, sounding a little surprised that you'd ask. She gives you St. James's phone number. You realize that you shouldn't make this call on your own line and tell Fawn you're going for a coffee. You buy a phone card from the news kiosk outside the building and walk a couple of blocks until you find a pay phone that's a suitable distance from the office. You dial John St. James's number.

E 15 ↑1.75 ADLAC 22 ↓2.60 ENE 50.50 ↑1.50 TYC 60.25 ↓1.75 MSO 65 ↑2

Go page 54.

"You can't fire me. Who do you think you are?" Barry spits at you. "And who the fuck are you?" he says, looking at Flaxworthy. "My replacement?" He looks like a marionette controlled by a drunken puppeteer. "I wouldn't work for this guy," he says, pointing at you, with spittle landing all over the front of Flaxworthy's striped tie. "He's as corrupt as they come."

"Barry, you're drunk," you say. "You don't know what you're saying. Maybe you should go home for the day. And I didn't fire you. But really, you should sleep this off before you say something you really regret."

"What about the missing money?" Barry says. "Moneyhouse knows about it. He knows what Weiss has been up to. We have to do what he asks, or we'll all go to jail."

Flaxworthy is suddenly interested. "Moneyhouse? What's this got to do with Moneyhouse? And who the hell is Weiss?"

"Weiss is our accountant," you say. "And don't listen to Barry. He's drunk. And confused."

"Like hell I am," says Barry. "What's so confusing about one-point-five billion dollars in hidden losses? Seems pretty straightforward to me. Where is Weiss? Let's just ask him now so your Tinky Winky friend here can get the real story."

"Gentlemen, I'm not sure what's going on here, but there are clearly a lot of questions about Fleece that need to be answered," says Flaxworthy, regaining his composure. "I'm going to have to call the enforcement division of the SEC and have a task force get to this office before the day is out."

Barry suddenly realizes what he's done and collapses in a heap against Fawn's desk, knocking her out of her chair in the process. There's a crash as her coffee mug shatters on the ground. And then there's an even louder crash. But this time, it's coming from behind your office door.

↑ 1.75 ADLAC 22 ↓ 2.60 ENE 50.50 ↑ 1.50 TYC 60.25 ↓ 1.75 MSO 65 ↑ 2.50

Go to page 195.

"Diane, baby, whatever you want. I'll have Carson call you when he's done here. Do whatever you want to the room—anything at all. But don't get rid of that painting of the mallards flying over the canoe. I love that thing."

"Oh, baby. That's why I love you so much. Anything? Really?"

"Yes, baby, anything."

It takes several minutes to get off the phone. The last thing you feel like doing is spending the afternoon listening to Diane yammer on about interior design, so you make your excuses and watch *How to Get Ahead in Advertising* on cable instead.

A couple of hours later you get another phone call. There's static on the line. You think it's Diane again. "Diane? Diane, is that you?"

"No, it's Victor Alvarez calling from Stanley."

The line is full of static, you realize, because he's calling from the Falkland Islands. You've been secretly funding Alvarez in violation of the US policy on stem cell research. He's experimenting with cloning sheep to create a genetically superior wool fiber that not only repels water but also rises in temperature when it comes in contact with water. The sheep have the added bonus of having the most lustrous wool in the Western Hemisphere.

"Things are fabulous down here," he says. "You have to come and meet Juanita."

"I'll be on the Monday morning flight out of JFK," you say, hanging up the phone.

Your wife and daughter arrive home bearing a Sherpa's load of shopping bags. You try to hide in the den, but there's a knock on the door and Apple comes in. She's got one hand behind her back.

"I have a present for you, Daddy." She pulls her hand out from behind her back and hands you a light blue box.

What could she have bought for you from Tiffany? You untie

the white silk ribbon and open the box. There's a chamois of the same color inside it. You pick it up and the gift slips into your hand, pricking your thumb on the way. It's a sterling silver fishing lure.

"It's called the Silver Fish. It reminded me of when we used to go fishing together up at the lake when I was small."

You get up and hug your daughter, truly touched by this rare moment of nostalgic generosity. She's the best thing that ever happened to you.

↑ 1.75 ADLAC 22 ↓ 2.60 ENE 50.50 ↑ 1.50 TYC 60.25 ↓ 1.75 MSO 65 ↑ 2.50

Go to page 193.

Just then a voice behind you says, "Hey-hey, boss man. Aren't you totally psyched?"

You turn, keeping Flaxworthy in sight out of the corner of your eye. It's the intern. That short, chubby guy with the goatee, the son of some guy in the human resources department. Josh? Jared? What the hell is his name again?

"Jared?"

"No, sir, it's Josh," he says. "I have a question for you. Do interns get stock in the company? I've been here for three weeks and was wondering when I get my first grant. You said at that meeting last week that Fleece will share the wealth with every employee. I really want to work here full-time after I graduate, which would make me an employee then, for sure. So aren't I one now, technically?"

You look at Josh and then turn and look back toward Flaxworthy. He's staring at you. You realize that Josh has started speaking again—his mouth is moving—but you're not listening to him. You hear the words "boat," "interest rate," and "hot blonde," but you're not processing any of it. You're looking at Flaxworthy, and he's frowning.

Who the hell is he talking to? you think. *Is it about us? Does he know about Weiss? Why did I lie to him about Barry? Oh God, I'm going to jail for fraud. All because of that punk Weiss.* You're still sweating and can feel your shirt stuck to your back.

Flaxworthy hangs up his phone. Josh has stopped speaking and appears to be waiting for some sort of response. "Why don't you call Fawn and set up a lunch date with me," you say. "We can discuss these issues in depth. But run along now, Jared. As you can see, I have a visitor."

Flaxworthy opens the conference room door. He seems deadly serious. If he was actually talking about you on the phone, he certainly doesn't seem to be happy about what he heard.

E 15 ↑1.75 ADLAC 22 ↓2.60 ENE 50.50 ↑1.50 TYC 60.25 ↓1.75 MSO 65 ↑2

Do you come clean now, tell him everything you know, and try to avert corporate and personal disaster? Go to page 21.

Or do you hope that Flaxworthy wasn't talking about you at all, and continue with the cover-up? Go to page 236.

Homer is dead. He drove his truck into a lake and drowned. Your team forfeits the next game, against Red's will, and they lose the remaining eleven games of the season.

Your fate unravels much like your team's. Except for a surge of "sympathy" buys of Homer's jersey, sales of Argonauts' clothing slows to a crawl. The board of directors reverses its earlier position and at Jason Homer's grave site, Henderson delivers the ultimatum that you sell the team and repay the debt to TownGroup immediately.

"Fuck off, Henderson. Show some respect here," you say out of respect for Homer, but also because you know he's right and you can't bear the thought of being separated from the Argonauts. You know, however, that if you don't comply, you'll be out of Fleece too. You are in a world of shit because of that class-A moron.

You end up selling the Argonauts for $200 million less than you bought the team for, to a Manhattan real estate developer and casino owner who changes the name of the team back to the Corporals. To pay the difference back to TownGroup and relieve Fleece of the burden of your debt, you have to sell all of your stock.

For a brief instant, out of all the employees of Fleece, you own the least amount of stock. Even Fawn owns more shares in Fleece than you. The only money you have now is what you get from your salary as CEO and senior designer.

You become that guy at the end of your local bar who gets drunk every Sunday afternoon in the fall and roots against the Corporals.

The end

You ride back to your office with an enormous weight on your shoulders. You arrive at 666 Madison Avenue, wondering what curveball is going to be thrown at you next.

The answer is sitting outside your office. A svelte, striking woman with long blond hair and a dark double-breasted pin-striped suit. She looks like the evil Nazi woman from the movies who leaves her victims wondering, *Is she going to torture me or fuck me?*

Fawn jumps up from behind her desk, knocking over her halogen arm lamp with her head as she rises. She is definitely rattled by the presence of this obviously powerful woman. "Good morning," Fawn says, lifting the lamp back into a standing position. "This woman is here to see you. She's been here for an hour."

The woman stands up. "Hello, my name is Beatrice Sutinis. Mr. Moneyhouse asked me to report to work here today. I'm the replacement for the accountant whom you let go."

Jesus, Moneyhouse works fast. You just left his office half an hour ago. How could you have already let Weiss go? You were actually considering just reassigning him to a branch office or something. Guess that's out.

Just then you notice Ms. Sutinis stubbing out a cigarette on the sole of her shoe. She then puts it in her handbag.

"Why . . . hello, Beatrice. I'm pleased to meet you. Won't you come into my office. . . ."

"You can call me Ms. Sutinis," she says, standing up.

"Of course, of course," you say, a little flabbergasted by her formidableness. "Please, Ms. Sutinis, let's step inside."

She follows you into your office, and you shut the door behind you.

≡ 15 ↑ 1.75 ADLAC 22 ↓ 2.60 ENE 50.50 ↑ 1.50 TYC 60.25 ↓ 1.75 MSO 65 ↑ 2.

Go to page 198.

Three days later you and Apple are leaning against a fence at a ranch in the Falkland Islands. "I can't believe I'm telling you this," you say to her, in the midst of a not-very-successful father-daughter heart-to-heart. "When I was in high school, I had sex with a substitute teacher. Bad idea. The point is, as a teenager, you have to make all these judgment calls. And it seems like there's no one to trust for advice. But I guess that's what being a teenager is all about. You're going to make some bad calls every once in a while, but you and I, we just need to be more open with each other."

You hope you've gotten through to her about making smart decisions, but you know—deep in your heart—that she isn't listening to you. Her gaze is stuck on Alvarez as he swaggers toward the two of you.

You've taken Apple along to the Falklands as a bonding exercise. But she seems to have fallen for Alvarez rather than your own fatherly charm. Alvarez is easily ten years older than you, but he is a fit and lean man with salt-and-pepper hair and horse saddle skin. He wears cowboy boots not because he thinks they're stylish, but because he's a real cowboy.

"Sir, Apple, I'm pleased to introduce you to Juanita."

You look down and find yourself staring at the most beautiful sheep you've ever seen in your life, blindingly white and soft as smoke. Juanita is a genetically modified sheep with the best wool that RNA could have woven. You plan to create the Cozy Couture line, which will serve as the sister to Silk Armor. Designed to be stylish in appearance and homey in feel, you can wear the clothes to a fancy dinner and then sleep in them as pajamas that night. Cozy Couture will help fulfill your dream— the complete clothing line, something for everybody.

Apple puts her hand on Juanita. "She's beautiful, and so soft," she says, looking into Alvarez's eyes. Alvarez pulls off his canteen and unscrews the top.

"Hold out your hand, Apple." She does and Alvarez pours

water over her palm very slowly. "Now pet her again."

Apple trustingly places her hand on the sheep's back. "Oh my God! It's warming up! This is so cool."

"It's warm," you interject, "never hot, right, Victor?"

"Never hot. It's perfect and ready for mass production. And, just so you know, we shaved this bushy beast five hours ago. The enhanced follicle genetics makes the hair grow back seventy-two times faster than a normal sheep. You'll never run out of wool."

"She's like a living factory," whispers Apple, her eyes darting up from the sheep's face to Alvarez's smile.

15 ↑1.75 ADLAC 22 ↓2.60 ENE 50.50 ↑1.50 TYC 60.25 ↓1.75 MSO 65 ↑2.

Go to page 221.

You push open your office door, only to see all the papers on your desk getting sucked out of a broken window across the room. Weiss is nowhere to be seen.

"Fawn, did Weiss leave my office?"

"No," she says, and starts to cry.

Together, you and Flaxworthy run to the window and look down. There's a mass of people gathering around the gruesome carcass of your erstwhile accountant. It almost looks like he dove headfirst.

When you finally tear yourself away from the window, you turn and see Flaxworthy picking up a piece of paper that was weighted down by what appears to be a key. Flaxworthy is reading the contents of the paper.

"It's a suicide note," he says.

"Let me see that," you say, trying to grab the piece of paper from him. But he steps back quickly and says, "See with your eyes, not with your hands. Here, let me read it to you." He holds the paper out in front of him and begins to read. . . .

5 ↑1.75 ADLAC 22 ↓2.60 ENE 50.50 ↑1.50 TYC 60.25 ↓1.75 MSO 65 ↑2.50

Go to page 102.

You decide after a month to take Laufetter out for your first real public appearance together—Pavarotti's last performance at the Met. You figure that there won't be too many paparazzi there—London Marriott and Nikki Poorie begin filming their reality show about working for the NYC Sanitation Department that evening—and that most of the people will be friendly to Sally.

During Luciano's second encore, there's a knock at your box. You ignore it. This is, after all, a historic moment, and your eyes are welling up with tears. The crowd in the front row of the mezzanine has unfurled a banner that reads WE LOVE YOU LUCIANO, and you find yourself thinking that yes, you do love Luciano. But the knocking gets louder. Someone is banging on the box door, and the crowd starts to turn and look your way. Even Pavarotti seems to have heard the banging and is staring up into the darkness above him. You stand up, annoyed, and go back and unlock the door.

"What the hell do you—"

A short, bald man in a cheap raincoat hands you a manila envelope. "You've been served. Have a nice evening." He turns and walks away. But cameras are already flashing in your direction.

NEW YORK POST
FLEECE CEO'S WIFE TO TAKE HIM TO THE CLEANERS!

DAILY NEWS
SWAN SONG FOR PAVAROTTI, FLEECE CEO

DRUDGE REPORT
FLEECE CEO CRIES WHEN SERVED WITH DIVORCE PAPERS

Go to page 124.

You belong to the exclusive Reebok Sports Club, where everybody who's anybody sweats and grunts in style. Unfortunately the supply closet back at work was short on workout apparel. You're wearing small yellow running shorts and an orange tank top. The combo makes you look like a piece of candy corn, and you try to work through the embarrassment on the elliptical machine.

You're watching the TV hanging above the machines through your sweat-soaked eyeballs. *The View* is on, and one of the women on the show is interviewing the cast of the reality show *Who's the Daddy?* Five guys and one woman are sequestered in a house for nine months, and they have to figure out who impregnated the woman. At first you're disgusted by the idea, but then you feel a twinge of connection with these people—a sense of brotherhood with your fellow reality stars. They're not so bad. Just because these five guys had sex with the same woman who is about to give birth to a bastard child doesn't make them bad people. It makes them different. Eccentric. And who are we to judge them?

You drift into a daydream of yourself on *The View* talking to Barbara Walters, saying how much harder, but more fun, the show was than you thought it would be. The daydream continues through your sauna session. Looking at a taut blond woman across from you in the co-ed sauna, it occurs to you how ironic it is that Tiffany is the actress but you're the one who's going to end up on TV. You wonder if she'll see the humor in the situation.

Then it hits you: The best person to make your dream a reality is the one person in this world you can't stand. The one person in your professional life who treated you like a jerk—Stu Kovacs.

5 ↑ 1.75 ADLAC 22 ↓ 2.60 ENE 50.50 ↑ 1.50 TYC 60.25 ↓ 1.75 MSO 65 ↑ 2.50

Go to page 171.

The conversation with Ms. Sutinis is unlike any you've had as a chief executive. Before it even starts, however, she pulls out a pack of Dunhill Blues and lights up.

"Ms. Sutinis, if you don't mind, this is a nonsmoking office."

"Really?" she says, looking straight at you. But she doesn't put it out.

You're not going to fight this battle right now. You've got more important things to deal with. Before long she's running the discussion, telling you what assistants she will need you to hire, what kind of office she wants, and, of course, that she'll need an Aeron chair for her back and a feng shui expert on call to make sure her work environment is always in balance.

You're interrupted by a pounding on your office door. "Boss! I need to talk to you." It's Weiss. Without waiting for an answer, he opens the door and stomps into your office.

"So you're the one," he says, looking at Sutinis. "My replacement?" He turns to you. "Good of you to tell me that you'd fired me. I had to hear it from Fawn, who just told me that she was going to miss my lemon squares."

"Weiss, Weiss, please," you say. "You haven't been fired . . . yet." Sutinis is sitting there, looking like she is already disappointed in your lack of spine. You turn toward her.

"Ms. Sutinis, why don't you go talk to Fawn, and she'll set you up with your office. In fact, she can get you anything you need." You motion toward the door. Thank God she takes the suggestion.

"Nice to meet you, Mr. Weiss," she says as she pulls the door shut behind her.

15 ↑1.75 ADLAC 22 ↓2.60 ENE 50.50 ↑1.50 TYC 60.25 ↓1.75 MSO 65 ↑2.

Go to page 68.

The trip to Grand Central is a failure. Every single man is wearing a blue shirt and a red tie, and all the women are wearing those horrible boots, Uggs, which are ugly on any person in any season. As you sit in your cab on the way home, you wonder if every day of being public will be this exhausting.

When you arrive, your wife greets you wearing a Pucci housedress. "Honey, I need you to look at the plans for the new kitchen," she says. "It's going to be very Rocco DiSpirito." You try to smile and act agreeable, but soon find yourself hiding in your den, watching SportsCenter without really watching it. You're trying to find a rationalization for the momentous decision you made this afternoon.

At 7:30 P.M. your teenage daughter, Apple, pokes her head in the door. She's holding a video camera in her hand. "Daddy, I'm going to sleep over at Jenny's tonight. Look at the new camera that Mom let me buy today! It's high-def and can wirelessly transmit to my computer. We're going to make a short film for class."

"That's great, honey," you say without looking up. "Just be careful on the subway with that."

"I'm not taking the subway, Dad. Mom says we can use a car service from now on." She laughs as she closes the door again.

You doze off, only realizing that you've been asleep when your cell phone rings.

"Hello," you say, disguising the sleepiness in your voice.

"I forgot to tell you something," says a male voice on the other end of the line, without introducing himself. It's Moneyhouse. "We've filed the papers to have me nominated to your board. Now let's talk about who else I want on it."

That never even occurred to you. Your board, like that of most private companies, is stuffed full of your college buddies and a few Fleece insiders like Barry. Even your wife is on it.

"Of course, of course," you say, lying. "I was going to call you about that tomorrow. I was wondering whether you had any suggestions."

"Of course I do," says Moneyhouse. "Let's start with the compensation committee. My time is precious, and if I'm going to be attending board meetings at Fleece, I'm going to need to be paid for it."

Go to page 145.

"Hello," you say into the phone.

"What an opening!" says a voice on the other end of the line. "You looked good up there ringing the bell, too. Yes, yes, you looked quite good indeed. This is J. P. Moneyhouse the fifth."

You're startled. Moneyhouse, after all, is the chairman of Moneyhouse and Stonecutter, the preeminent Wall Street investment bank. You've read stories about the man, but even with your own level of modest success, you never thought you'd actually be getting a call from him.

He's the sort of person whom you can't imagine ever having been a child, as if his life began at the age of fifty. Bald on top with white tufts on each side of his head, he has a bulbous nose that looks more like a gourd than anything human. His mustache hangs bushy over his mouth, giving him the appearance of a constant frown. (You always thought he looked like that hippie caddie on the PGA Tour.) Mr. Moneyhouse has never been accused by any of his rivals of stabbing anyone in the back. He prefers, it is said, to stab them right through the heart.

"What can I do for you, Mr. Moneyhouse?" you say. "You know, I'm quite busy today."

"It's more like what I can do for you," says Moneyhouse. "It's the same with all you young bucks. You think you've invented business by the way you act once you've gone public. But you do realize, it's only just beginning. I'm calling to offer you the services of Moneyhouse and Stonecutter. Now that you're public, and will be buying companies and selling securities on a regular basis, you're going to need the services of a real investment bank, not that Podunk outfit you've been using until now. Why don't you drop by the Mercantile for a three-martini lunch? We've got lots to talk about."

"Why, that's a capital idea," you reply, wincing as you realize you're pouring it on a little too thick trying to impress him. "How about I see you there in an hour?"

"Excellent," he says. "At my usual table."

You hang up your cell phone and yell through your door. "Fawn, get Barry on his cell." Barry McTeagle is your corporate counsel, and also your closest friend from the University of Virginia. You met him when he broke down the door to your dorm room in a drunken stupor thinking he was locked out of his own room.

When your office phone beeps, you pick it up. "Barry, meet me at the Mercantile in an hour. We're meeting Moneyhouse."

15 ↑1.75 ADLAC 22 ↓2.60 ENE 50.50 ↑1.50 TYC 60.25 ↓1.75 MSO 65 ↑2.

Go to page 143.

The next eight weeks are a blur. Not only are you still running a public company, but you are also flying back and forth to LA to look at casting tapes. You're also taking voice lessons, and you've even installed a full gym in your office. Stu's twist on the reality genre was that your show would be aired as close to live as possible. What you tape in any given week will be on air the next, giving a sense of real time to the viewer at home.

You lose fifteen pounds thanks to constant exercise and the Melrose diet that Stu has you on, which allows you to eat only cottage cheese and melon. Your exercise regimen has reinvigorated your love life with your wife and you haven't thought about Tiffany in weeks. The camera crew actually busted the two of you making love in your shower, and it took your threatening to walk off the project to get that tape back from Stu.

You ultimately collect twelve "designers" to put through the ringer. Only six of them are actually designers and the other half are out-of-work actors and B-level models. Ironically the first two people whom you let go are actual designers. You've even found a catchphrase when giving them the kiss-off, which sweeps the country by storm: "You can't cut it."

Your office is a mess, but business is booming. Employees from Fleece are split down the middle regarding how they feel about the cameras' presence. Some have quit in protest; others have gotten face-lifts and new wardrobes to look their best on the show. Sales are up on your clothing line. You've made a deal with Target to fill their racks with Silk Armor. The chain even adapted your catchphrase to use as the slogan for the clothing line: "The price is so low, we can't cut it."

5 ↑ 1.75 ADLAC 22 ↓ 2.60 ENE 50.50 ↑ 1.50 TYC 60.25 ↓ 1.75 MSO 65 ↑ 2.50

Go to page 165.

The judge sentences you to five months in prison and five months of house arrest. You head for the courthouse steps to give the prepared speech you were praying not to have to use. A huge crowd has assembled.

"I'd like to make a brief statement. This is a shameful day. It's shameful for me and my family, for my beloved company, and for the apparel industry in general. What was a small personal matter became an almost fatal circus event of unprecedented proportions. I have been choked and almost suffocated to death during that time.

"I would like to thank everybody who stood by me, who wished me well, waved to me on the street, smiled at me, called me, wrote to me. Especially the flock who have been camped out on the courthouse steps dressed as sheep. You guys are amazing. [The flock lets out a unified "BAA!"] Perhaps all of you out there can continue to show your support by buying our products. And whatever happened to me personally shouldn't have any effect whatsoever on the great company Fleece Industries. And I don't want to use this as a sales pitch for my company, but we love that company. And we really think it merits great attention from the American public.

"And I'll be back. I will be back. Whatever I have to do in the next few months, I hope the months go by quickly. I'm not afraid. I'm not afraid whatsoever. I'm just very sorry that a small personal matter has been blown out of all proportion, and with such venom and such gore. I mean, it's just terrible."

You stop there and wait for the crowd to cheer. But they just laugh at you.

The end

You lean back in your chair and stare at the painting of Moneyhouse III, looking for some answers in the brushstrokes depicting a legend and wondering how on earth it came to this. You thought you did everything right. You built up your own business from scratch. You hired people you knew were reliable, industrious, and honest. Half of major league baseball wears Silk Armor and you don't even pay them!

Now everything is slipping away. But you will not be brought down by the hubris of an employee. The company is bigger than this. Your vision is bigger than anything.

Moneyhouse is right—your options are really just two: try to cover this thing up (what to do with Weiss is an open question) or start packing your valise for a long trip to the slammer. The answer couldn't be more obvious.

At that very moment, the waiter arrives with a round of drinks. As he hands you yours, you put on your best smile and say, "Here's to a long-lasting—and lucrative—union. I'd be honored to join your rarified roster of clients." Barry, who was looking like he was about to have a heart attack, exhales audibly and reaches for his own glass. Moneyhouse doesn't even flinch—clearly he's been through this before. The three of you raise your glasses in unison. You bring yours to your lips and feel the vodka slide down your throat into a stomach that contains nothing but the morning's champagne. You realize you're going to have to stock up the liquor cabinet at home.

After all, you've just crossed the line.

5 ↑ 1.75 ADLAC 22 ↓ 2.60 ENE 50.50 ↑ 1.50 TYC 60.25 ↓ 1.75 MSO 65 ↑ 2.5

Go to page 234.

You quickly locate the number of Felix Filippo, your broker at TownGroup, and dial it.

"I haven't heard from you in ages," he says. "But that's probably because the dividends alone from your Fleece stock are too much money to know what to do with. What can I do for you?"

"Listen, Felix, I need to know how many shares of Fleece I have in my account at TownGroup."

"Ten million, same as always given that you've never sold a single one. But that doesn't include the ones from your stock grant that you invested with that guy in DC."

"I need you to sell five million of those shares," you tell him. "Today. Can you get that done?" You think to yourself that five million shares just might be enough to squeak under regulators' radars.

"Five million? That's almost seventy million dollars' worth of Fleece. Why? Are you getting fired or something? You do know it's going to put heavy pressure on the price, don't you?" he says, though you can tell he's greedily calculating how much he'll make on commissions from this one trade alone.

"Just do it, Felix. No reason, really. I just need some liquidity right now. The wife's clamoring for a Tuscan villa, and I've been eyeing this sweet little private jet."

"Okay, fine. I'll do it. Oh, Barry left a message for me yesterday to call him about his own account. Think he'd be interested in knowing the boss is selling his shares, if you know what I mean?"

You're caught in a bind. If Barry finds out you're doing this without telling him, he'll be enraged. On the other hand, the more shares that trade today, the greater the likelihood that the Securities and Exchange Commission will be hot on the trail.

15 ↑1.75 ADLAC 22 ↓2.60 ENE 50.50 ↑1.50 TYC 60.25 ↓1.75 MSO 65 ↑2.5

Should you help Barry out? After all, Barry's the one who told you. Shouldn't you return the favor? Go to page 103.

Or do you tell Felix to keep quiet about your sale? It's your own business, and Barry can take care of himself. Go to page 66.

"You know, Red, I don't think I want to be that aggressive with my money when I'm just learning the ropes here," you say.

He slams his binder shut, stands up, and starts walking to the door. "Goddamn corporate owners," he mutters. "Don't know a goddamn thing about football. Just want to hang out with star athletes, pick the cheerleaders, and talk to the press."

"Hold it right there, Red," you say. "What you say is somewhat true—especially the part about the cheerleaders—but let's not forget something. I'm a businessman, and this is a business. You're my employee. If you want to keep your job, I'd suggest you learn a few basics of authority. It's a bad idea to mouth off to the boss. You may be in charge of a bunch of kids out there on the field, but I sign your paycheck. If you want to keep getting one, you'll learn to pay me the respect I have earned. I invented bulletproof clothing, for Christ's sake. I'm no flash in the pan."

"Let me tell you something as well," he replies defiantly. "Running a sports team means you've got to know when to make moves. You might have a bulletproof defensive line one season, and for no apparent reason, it will be as porous as a sieve the next. You can be on top of the world today and be the laughingstock of the league tomorrow. If you don't do something to help me improve this team, you're going to have to start wearing those bulletproof clothes of yours to the games. The fans are just about ready to kill all of us."

He slams the door as he leaves.

What a prick, you think. *If we lose our next game, I'll do as he says and make a move. I'll fire him.*

5 ↑ 1.75 ADLAC 22 ↓ 2.60 ENE 50.50 ↑ 1.50 TYC 60.25 ↓ 1.75 MSO 65 ↑ 2.50

Go to page 215.

The limo pulls up at 85 Broad Street, legendary home of Moneyhouse and Stonecutter. Several doormen come streaming toward the car, their coats flapping like cordial wraiths, and before you know it, you've literally been carried into the building and escorted up to the thirty-fourth floor, where the executive conference rooms are found.

You follow Moneyhouse through double doors into a room that seems, as far as your limited design knowledge is concerned, to be decorated in London mustachio. To your surprise, Weiss is sitting at the table between two accountant types with mountains of paper stacked up on either side of him. *How is it that all my employees get where I'm going before I do?* you think. Weiss looks up at you, and his face is ashen. "Hi, boss," he mumbles. "Really, I thought it would all work out in the end. I'm sorry."

You can't bear to look at him. Moneyhouse, apparently feeling your pain, puts his arm around you. "Here's what my boys here are telling me," he says. "What Weiss has done is camouflage approximately one-point-five billion in losses over the past four years."

You didn't believe it when he first said it, but now he's saying it again—$1.5 billion? How could that have happened?

"Not to worry, though," says Moneyhouse. "We think we've figured a way out of this mess: an off–balance sheet entity headquartered in Nigeria that will buy and sell barges. If Fleece funds forty-nine percent of it and we gather investments for the other fifty-one percent, you won't even have to show the losses in your financial statements."

"Wait," you say, "that sounds illegal. That's the kind of thing that destroys companies. Aren't we just digging a deeper hole? We're in the clothing business; I don't see how that relates to African barges."

"As of today, those barges are more important than any scrap of clothing you have ever designed," says Moneyhouse. "But let me finish. We can easily raise that fifty-one percent by offering people a guaranteed return. Say, five hundred percent on their original investment. In the grand scheme of things, it will be well worth it. That way, we can move the losses into the Nigerian company, clean up Fleece's own income statement, and no one will be the wiser. Simple as saying, 'Let's do it.' So what do you say? Shall we dance?"

5 ↑ 1.75 ADLAC 22 ↓ 2.60 ENE 50.50 ↑ 1.50 TYC 60.25 ↓ 1.75 MSO 65 ↑ 2.50

Do you say yes, and hide the losses in an offshore company? Go to page 219.
Or do you decide that this has gone on long enough, and prepare to accept whatever punishment your own ignorance has led you to deserve? Go to page 223.

The next few months are surprisingly stress-free. The camera crew takes an instant liking to Tiffany, so whenever they're not following you, they are invariably in the mailroom or following Tiffany on her rounds. And Tiffany makes sure that the camera remains focused on her. She wears microminis and pushes the mail cart around the office like a cigarette girl working the room in an old nightclub. Male employees stop work five minutes before their scheduled mail delivery to comb their hair and floss their teeth, often huddling to swap fantasies with one another like teenage boys.

After a couple of weeks of giving you the cold shoulder, Fawn reverts to her former self, having apparently decided that Tiffany is more interested in getting in front of the camera than in getting into your pants—or Fawn's chair. You barely even see Tiffany yourself, and instead focus on the show, the company, and your family (in that order).

But Fawn is only partly right about Tiffany. One evening in early December, after the camera crews have left for the day, you hear a quiet knock on your door.

"Yes?"

"It's me. Tiffany."

"Um . . . come in," you say, desperately hoping no one sees her come into your office.

She opens the door, slips in, and says, "There's no one else here. I just delivered the last mail round of the day, and I swear, there's not a soul in this office. It kind of freaked me out. And then it made me horny."

You stand up. "Tiff, you know the deal we made . . . you'd get the job and some time on camera—God knows, you've gotten enough of that—but as far as you and I are concerned, it's over. . . ."

She starts untying her smock. "Oh, please. Don't you want a little of what you've been missing these last few weeks?" She takes her smock off, and she's wearing only a canary yellow miniskirt.

"Come to Papa," you say.

An hour and a half later, you're sitting in a car on your way home. Like any man in your position, you'd succumbed to Tiffany's advances. But you told her afterward that it wouldn't happen again. If she tried, you'd have to fire her. There's just too much at risk for both of you. She agreed but sneered at you, saying that you weren't enough of a man for her anyway, and informed you that she was moving in with one of the cameramen once the season was over.

"That's great news, Tiffany," you said, trying not to sound jealous. "Things are going really well with my wife, anyway."

You weren't lying to Tiffany. Things *are* going well with your wife. She's taken to the peripheral fame she's gained by being on the show, and even occasionally goes to chat rooms on AOL to see if people are talking about what she wore on such and such an episode. While the sex is nothing like it is with Tiffany, it's most certainly adequate, especially given how tired you usually are when you get home.

In fact, everything is going well in your life. Good marriage, good friends, *The Simple Stitch* is the number-one reality show in the country, and everyone in the world wants to dress like "Harry."

You decide that the reality show has run its course and you have accomplished what you set out to do. Your brand, Harry, is a household name, and you are richer and more famous than you ever thought you could be when you started as a junior designer living in an East Village studio apartment so many years ago. ("I lived in Alphabet City before it was cool," is a line you often use.) After a long talk with your wife, you both decide that it's best not to re-up your show after this year so that you can enjoy your success in private.

Kovacs, of course, doesn't take the news too well. You hear something that sounds like a chair being thrown through the window of his office when you tell him. You are taking away the only number-one hit in this pathetic man's whole mediocre career. He eventually calms down, however, and gets you to agree to let him run an extra hour of outtakes, interviews, and bloopers after the final episode. "I'll make a few million from that alone, which will be enough to soothe my damaged feelings," he tells you. Whatever. A few million? Fleece stock has been on fire of late, as investors have decided that the brand Harry is one to bet on. A few million is pocket change to you, but if the blooper show will get that prick Kovacs out of the picture, you're all for it.

You're sitting with your wife and daughter in front of the television as the last show of the season unfolds. They'd made you promise not to tell anyone which of the final contestants—Bernadette, an Estonian fashion model with a hoop nose ring, or Trevor, a metrosexual with a sassy attitude—had won, as they wanted it to be a surprise. Apple has invited a few friends over as well, and for the first time since she turned twelve, you're getting the feeling that she actually thinks you're cool again.

E 15 ↑ 1.75 ADLAC 22 ↓ 2.60 ENE 50.50 ↑ 1.50 TYC 60.25 ↓ 1.75 MSO 65 ↑ 2

Go to page 91.

"Look, it's pretty simple," he says. "I came out. And that's fine. My wife wasn't thrilled, but at least now I can live my life honestly and stop skulking around. But clearly I can no longer own a football team. Imagine me trying to go into the locker room. These guys, although some of the most perfect physical specimens you will ever see, are also the most intellectually retarded group of people on the planet. They can't handle someone like me. I don't fit into their idea of a perfect universe. I have to sell the team. And I figured that since we were having lunch anyway, I'd give you the first shot at an offer. Think about it: Not only could you outfit them in Fleece sportswear, but you could also turn the entire thing into a Fleece promotion. I only want six hundred million."

You know deep down that you shouldn't be in the business of buying a sports team. And neither should Fleece; the board of directors would never go for it. But you really want this, even though the Corporals have a dismal 0-and-3 record.

You think, *Maybe I'm done with clothes. I've conquered one industry and it's time to explore new horizons. Every mogul buys a sports team at one point in his life. And if the recent wave of tech nerds investing in sports teams is any indication, I clearly don't have to know anything about sports to own a team.*

Way back when you were starting out in your small private company, you established an arrangement whereby you could personally take advances off the company's line of credit. You haven't taken advantage of that credit line in years, but now seems like the perfect time. You could buy the Corporals independently of Fleece and pay back the loan with the earnings you will make off the team, or by selling some of your Fleece shares. Owning a sports team? That would certainly cement your reputation as a corporate swashbuckler.

↑1.75 ADLAC 22 ↓2.60 ENE 50.50 ↑1.50 TYC 60.25 ↓1.75 MSO 65 ↑2.50

Do you borrow $600 million using Fleece's credit line to buy the Corporals? Go to page 64.

Or do you stick with what you know—clothing? After all, $600 million is more than a trifle. Go to page 130.

You stare at the umbrella stand as you consider how to talk her out of this. You notice that the monkey has enormous balls and you can't believe how much this monstrosity cost. "Diane. Diane. Come on, baby. You don't really want to redecorate that room, do you? When we're there together, we don't even notice the decor, except maybe the chandelier over the bed."

"Yeah, but I spend a lot of time in that room when you're not there. And I'm tired of looking at an oil painting of mallards flying over a canoe while I wait for your phone call."

"It *is* a hotel room, we don't own it—it seems foolish to want to furnish it."

"It's a hotel room for you! But it's my home! You have a home that you get to decorate. You have a home where you can eat breakfast, walk on rugs you like, and sit on custom-made sofas."

"Diane, you're getting upset. I get the feeling we're not talking about furniture anymore."

"Go fuck yourself! Of course we're not talking about furniture. I'm tired of you giving everything to your wife and leaving me the scraps. I deserve better than this. I can go out and get any man I want to."

There comes a time in every affair when a tryst becomes a travesty of expectations.

"Maybe you should, Diane," you say, immediately regretting it. "I'm sorry. I didn't mean it. Let's meet and talk, okay? . . . Diane? Diane?"

E 15 ↑1.75 ADLAC 22 ↓2.60 ENE 50.50 ↑1.50 TYC 60.25 ↓1.75 MSO 65 ↑2

Go to page 18.

You fire Red the next week even though the Argonauts don't technically lose. Actually, in a precedent-setting move in the AFL, the team is disqualified from playing the game against the Oklahoma Spartans.

Nothing seems out of the ordinary at first. The stadium fills up for the first time all year, thanks to the new marketing campaign you launched: "Come set sail with the Argonauts! We're on a voyage to VICTORY!"

You're sitting in your new owner's box with your wife, Apple, Fawn, Jeff, and Araz. Araz is swallowing a bag of popcorn, still complaining about your decision not to sign Homer. "He's so sexy. Think of what he could have done for us in terms of image!"

"Araz, I thought I was the image of this company. If you've got such a problem with that, let me know. Maybe I can find some new marketing people."

"That's not what I meant, boss," he says. "It's just that you're no spring chicken. Homer is someone people want to look like. He's sexy, sassy, and in shape."

Suddenly the stadium's sound system announces the arrival of your opponents on the field. They come running out in that supercharged way that football players do—a bunch of oversize men all ready to blow their top at the same moment.

And finally, the moment you and everyone else are waiting for—the Argonauts are about to come out, in their new uniforms and under new ownership. The music you chose as the new team anthem—"Sharp Dressed Man" by ZZ Top—starts pounding, and the team starts charging out of the tunnel . . . naked. Every player on your new team comes onto the field bare-assed and screaming like the day they were born. Apple bursts out laughing. Araz is transfixed. You turn and throw a tray of crudités against the wall.

In the end, it turns out that Simpson had let the word out to the team that you'd decided not to hire Homer. He then got them all worked up about dressing in uniforms "designed by a couple of faggots on Madison Avenue," and they made a group decision to protest the new ownership. And your team was disqualified. They won't play again until you sell them, which you ultimately do for $400 million. The "New Corporals" then go on to pick up the star quarterback, Homer, and win the championship.

You go back to making clothes, sell most of your Fleece shares to pay back the rest of the loan, and never watch football again.

The end

You're beside yourself. Where is your phone? You've got to call your wife and call it all off. Just as you flip your cell open to dial her number, it rings. It's Diane.

Maybe she can come over and keep you company. Dan the doorman will give you the heads-up if the wife is on the way. Why not? That would be sweet revenge for the travesty that's entered your apartment today.

"Hello, baby. Daddy's lonely," you coo into the phone.

"Where are you, Sugar? I thought we were going to play some 'squash' today. Court three eighteen is open and ready." Diane is talking in her pillow voice. You're putty in her hands.

"Oh, Diane, I wish I could! I'm stuck at home accepting deliveries of some new home furnishings. It's crazy. My wife is in cahoots with Carson Rodriguez. They're trying to bankrupt me! Five-hundred-dollar pincushions and six-thousand-dollar shower curtains! I'm going apeshit!"

"You and your wife are redecorating your home?"

Uh-oh. Her voice has gone from the warmth of a shared bed to the chill of a prison cot.

You try to play it off. "She's excited, you know. It keeps her happy to have projects."

"Oh, I love a good project. Why don't you send Carson over to three eighteen—he'll do wonders for the place."

You're in a jam here. But you suddenly remember that you're not even paying for Carson. Fleece is. You can just add Diane to the bill if you have to.

↑1.75 ADLAC 22 ↓2.60 ENE 50.50 ↑1.50 TYC 60.25 ↓1.75 MSO 65 ↑2.50

Do you acquiesce and tell Diane she can have whatever she wants to preserve your romantic oasis? Go to page 188.

Or do you try and find another way to pacify her that won't end up costing Fleece another two hundred thousand dollars or so? Go to 214.

After the practice you're sitting in a room off a passageway in the stadium, talking to Simpson.

He is proposing another major financial commitment. The last-place Buzzards are shopping Jason Homer, the only Greek quarterback to ever make the AFL. And Simpson wants you to agree to Homer's demand for a $252 million contract.

"What about Fallow?" you ask.

"A second-stringer at best," he replies. "Have you not watched any of our first three games?"

"But two hundred and fifty-two million? Isn't that a bit rich, no matter who we're talking about?"

"He's a bargain at that rate," says Simpson. "And he's the most popular player in the country."

"Red, I need to think here. Two hundred and fifty-two million dollars. Christ, that could bankrupt me."

"You don't need all the money right away," he replies. "Just the ten million signing bonus. And think of what's going to happen to Fleece sales when you sign him. Every kid in the country will start wearing your clothes."

≡ 15 ↑1.75 ADLAC 22 ↓2.60 ENE 50.50 ↑1.50 TYC 60.25 ↓1.75 MSO 65 ↑2.

Do you go ahead and tell him to make the offer to Homer? Go to page 14.

Or do you tell him not to go for Homer—$252 million for one player is absurd. Go to page 207.

"I don't see that there's any other alternative," you say to Moneyhouse. "I assume you'll take the lead?"

"Of course." Moneyhouse is glowing. He's obviously in his element. "Everything will be taken care of," he continues. "All you need to do is go back to your office and issue the press release we're drafting that says Fleece is investing in forty-nine percent of the Nigerian barge company. We'll take care of the rest. You just get ready to respond to any calls from the press or from stock analysts. Tell them it's crucial to the company's interests that it gets a foothold in Africa. Hopefully, no one will ask any questions beyond that."

"What if they do?" you ask.

"People need sport clothes in Africa, too," he replies. "Also, I will obviously be needing a seat on the board of Fleece," he says. "The paperwork on that is also ready. If you'd sign here, that will all be taken care of." You're a little stunned but sign on the dotted line anyway.

The next thing you know, he's walked you out of the conference room and the door has been shut behind you. "A car is waiting for you downstairs," says a secretary, without looking up. "Have a nice day."

You take the elevator down, walk out of Moneyhouse and Stonecutter, and climb into the car. As you make your way back to 666 Madison Avenue, you take stock of the situation. *This is just a placeholder,* you think. *To make up for some fool's mistake. It's not like I'm robbing widows and orphans here. All we're doing is operating in the gray area of accounting. It's all a matter of interpretation anyway. I can't let Weiss bring down everything we've all worked for.*

Before you know it, you're back at your office. Fawn tells you that there's a fax for you from Moneyhouse and Stonecutter. "It's a press release," she says, handing it to you. You think to yourself that this could be easier than you first thought, especially if Moneyhouse is going to take care of everything. "Fawn, put this release on letterhead and send it to Business Wire and

Newswire immediately. I have some business to attend to," you say as you slam your office door.

As you sit down behind your desk, though, you realize that your mind is racing. You can't get any work done. You need to blow off some steam. You could do what you often do in this situation, and head to Grand Central Station. Standing on the western balcony and looking down at the aquarium of travelers, moving about on both business and pleasure, you get a chance to see what America is wearing—and how they like to wear it. Or you could just go see your mistress Diane in room 318 of the Pierre Hotel for a quick roll in the hay. You enjoy that, too.

E 15 ↑1.75 ADLAC 22 ↓2.60 ENE 50.50 ↑1.50 TYC 60.25 ↓1.75 MSO 65 ↑2

Do you go to Grand Central and do a little field research? Go to page 199. Or do you go see your lady who will be wearing no clothes at all? Go to page 39.

That night you have lamb for dinner. But not just any lamb. You're eating Juanita's genetic twin, Jesus. Cloned lamb meat. It's got a texture like velvet—the softest, most succulent meat you've ever put in your mouth. Apple asks Alvarez if it was cooked in mint, and he congratulates her on her discerning tongue. "Jesus was kept on a strict diet of fresh mint and spring water his entire life," he says. "It makes for a delicious meal, but we couldn't use him for wool. The side effect of the mint was that he turned green. We finally had to kill him when some of the other ranchers started suspecting something was up."

You spend the rest of the night drinking Falkland Islands gin. You even let Apple have a little—she's tipsy halfway through the glass, and making moon eyes at Alvarez.

The next morning is too bright and too loud for your gin-soaked brain as you and Apple roll into Alvarez's pick-up truck and take a bumpy ride to the airport. You board the plane and both you and Apple zonk out once you feel the plush leather of the first-class seats. Before you know it, you've landed at JFK.

After being herded through customs, you finally get into your waiting limo and check your messages. You have one. It's from Beatrice Sutinis.

"We should have a meeting when you get back. I will be in your office at ten A.M. tomorrow to chat about financials. Hope your flight was smooth."

She needs to get laid, you think. The rest of the limo ride is spent fielding questions from Apple about a summer abroad in the Falkland Islands. She says she really wants to get into stem cell research. But you know that the charm of a lonely cowboy lassoed her in.

You get home and Apple gives your wife the stuffed penguin that she bought in the Falkland Islands airport. You eat some Chinese takeout and go to sleep. As you slip into bed and feel the comfort of your brand-new $5,900 sheets, you think, *Why doesn't Fleece make sheets this exquisite?* And you drift off to sleep.

The next morning you get up early, surprisingly refreshed from your quick jaunt to the Southern Hemisphere. You arrive at your office by a quarter to nine—Fawn isn't even in yet—and push open your office door.

You're startled by the sight of Sutinis, sitting behind your desk, smoking a cigarette—what the . . . ? You're about to fire her when you notice somebody out of the corner of your eye. You turn toward your sofa. Moneyhouse.

"Welcome back," he says without smiling.

Go to page 227.

How am I going to do this? you ask yourself. After all, you've already seen evidence of Moneyhouse's tough side. Will you even be able to make it out of the building if you say no? You remember reading about the mysterious disappearance of Stonecutter several years ago after a company Christmas party. There were rumors that people in New Jersey had seen a Santa Claus floating downstream on the Hudson in the snow-reflected moonlight that night. Moneyhouse ended up with full control of the firm after Stonecutter's disappearance, and he has continually described the rumors of his involvement in his partner's vanishing as merely the rantings of envious wannabes.

"I'm feeling a little dizzy," you say. "I don't know if it's the drinks or all this bad news. Of course we can do it," you continue, "but I think I need to get some fresh air."

Moneyhouse frowns but says, "Of course, take your time. We have plenty to talk to Weiss about. Go down to the helipad and take in some nice ocean air. We'll expect you back in half an hour, yes?"

"Sure," you say, and move for the door. Out in the elevator bank, you grab the wall for support. You weren't lying about the light-headedness. You're about to call the cops and most likely destroy the company you've spent your entire life building. The elevator arrives, and you climb in and start your descent.

5 ↑ 1.75 ADLAC 22 ↓ 2.60 ENE 50.50 ↑ 1.50 TYC 60.25 ↓ 1.75 MSO 65 ↑ 2.50

Go to page 241.

The next six months are a blur. First, the police arrive, searching for Weiss's office for any suspicious signs. They don't find anything and conclude that he was just another wayward husband who kept his secret from everyone he knew. A month after that, the SEC shows up; given that Weiss was your accountant, they hunt for any reasons that he would have had to fly the coop. They don't find anything either. Apparently Sutinis knew what she was doing.

You're not an entirely evil person, so you ultimately get together with Phyllis and tell her you'll see to it that she's taken care of, given Weiss's contribution to Fleece over the years. She gets a divorce shortly after his disappearance and is remarried within two months to another researcher at her lab. The gossip around the office is that they both must have been having affairs. "It must have been a really unhappy marriage," you find yourself saying to Fawn one day as you lie in bed with her.

Sutinis's contribution to your cover-up doesn't stop with Weiss. She manufactures a gigantic earnings gain for the fourth quarter, and Fleece stock shoots through the roof.

Upon reflection when the storm passes, you decide that you made the right decision, even if it didn't really work out for Weiss. Your wife has begun having the whole house remodeled. The only thing that's been bothering you is John St. James. What did he do with the body? It never turned up, and, as instructed, he never called you again. It doesn't bother you every day, but it's there in the back of your mind. You know, deep down, that everything could still cave in on you.

One day, after returning from a meeting at the White House, where you presented the president with a custom-made Fleece golf outfit, you turn on the TV in your den to see if you can catch any coverage of yourself in the Oval Office. The first thing that shows up on the screen is a picture of a huge fire in Idaho, with a headline underneath: MILITIA MEMBER BLOWS HIMSELF UP WITH WAREHOUSE FULL OF PIPE BOMBS.

A mug shot of John St. James suddenly shows up onscreen. The news correspondent goes on to say that St. James had been building a stockpile of pipe bombs to finish what he started so many years ago—to blow up the IRS. But he's dead. And so is the only link connecting you to Weiss's death.

God bless this country, you think as you turn off the TV.

The end

Two months later you're sitting at the defense table at the New York District Court squeezed between Carson Rodriguez and your lawyer, Johnny Conran. Conran has a reputation for getting guilty guys off the hook, which makes his clients guilty by association just for hiring the man.

The courtroom is filled with reporters and sketch artists, who can't seem to draw you without a scowl on your face. The gallery is filled with die-hard consumers who cheer you on and spurned stockholders who want to see you sink as low as their retirement funds.

Carson, too, has people in the gallery cheering him on. During every court recess he goes into the bathroom and changes his wardrobe, "to keep with the mood of the day." You can't believe that you are even sharing a defense with him.

Sutinis is the prosecution's key witness. She has found fame as the honest whistleblower. She has appeared on all of the talk shows of every cable news network telling the world how important it is to take a risk, even if it means being ostracized.

"It's hard enough being a woman in a man's world," she explains. "Excluded from the corporate bonding get-togethers in strip clubs and golf outings, but to have to be the sole voice of reason and honesty?"

She also manages to get herself a lucrative book deal that details her exploits as she pulled the thread and unwove the corrupt sweater that was Fleece. She got a million-dollar advance and the best ghostwriter in the business. But now she is sitting in the witness stand wiping a tear from her eye as she explains that it's so hard to find honest work in a dishonest society.

15 ↑1.75 ADLAC 22 ↓2.60 ENE 50.50 ↑1.50 TYC 60.25 ↓1.75 MSO 65 ↑2.5

Go to page 40.

"Moneyhouse . . . what a surprise! What are you doing here? And if you don't mind my asking, Ms. Sutinis, what are you using for an ashtray?"

You notice your favorite coffee mug in front of her—Apple gave it to you for Father's Day when she was just a kid—#1 DAD. She takes a long drag off her Dunhill and drops it into the mug.

"We have to talk," says Moneyhouse. "Beatrice called me last night a little concerned over some expenses she uncovered going over the American Express online statements. Your daughter's ticket to the Falklands was in there. Not that big a deal, of course, but we can't have Fleece paying for your family vacations."

"Oh, of course. I'll pay for her ticket. It was last minute, and it was easy just to put both tickets on my card. It wasn't a vacation, by the way. We're doing some stem cell research down there. There's a sheep—its name is Juanita—and its wool will blow your mind."

"We know about Juanita," says Moneyhouse. "But that's not the end of it. After she saw that, she came across a bunch of bills from Carson Rodriguez. Terra-cotta in the office is one thing, but a four-hundred-and-forty-five-dollar pincushion? What the hell's that all about? Are you sewing your own clothes now?"

You can't believe that two people who didn't have a damn thing to do with Fleece until recently are here, in your own office, questioning you. You could throw them out right now. Then again, Moneyhouse is right: a $445 pincushion is really inexcusable.

15 ↑ 1.75 ADLAC 22 ↓ 2.60 ENE 50.50 ↑ 1.50 TYC 60.25 ↓ 1.75 MSO 65 ↑ 2.5

Go to page 128.

You can't believe it. What is she doing here? You haven't spoken to Tiffany in weeks. She called you a couple of times, but you were too busy to return the calls. She stopped trying to contact you, and you thought it was mutually agreed that your affair was over. Boy, were you wrong.

Tiffany runs over to you and gives you a big hug. "Hi, baby," she coos.

You turn around to the camera crew that's capturing all of this on tape. "Get out of here."

The cameraman keeps taping and says, "Mr. Kovacs said to get everything."

"Well, I say get away from me! If you want to keep your job, get out of here."

The cameraman leaves you alone with Tiffany, and the first thing that comes out of your mouth is, "What are you doing here?"

"Good to see you, too, asshole."

"I didn't mean it like that. I'm just surprised."

"How about a kiss, now that we're alone?" Tiffany pulls you to her by your lapels.

"I don't think it's good idea. There are cameras everywhere."

"That's what I want to talk to you about," she says. "Why didn't you put me in your show? I could be a designer. I was really hurt when you ignored my calls."

"Sorry about that. I was just swamped and, to be honest, I had no control over the casting. That was all Fox. And it's too late now. We've filmed almost half the season."

"No, it's not. You can hire me at Fleece. I've watched the show—those people get face time. Put me in that office and I'll make my own mark."

"I don't know, Tiff. It's pretty risky. What will the rest of the office say?"

"You know something? We had a good time together. Doesn't that mean anything to you? I thought you loved me, and I came here because I thought you'd want to help me. I understand if we can't fuck anymore, but I think the least you can do is help me get on TV."

She begins to cry. You look at Tiffany, still in awe of her beauty and now moved by her vulnerability. It occurs to you that if she doesn't press to rekindle your relationship, maybe the best move would be to hire her and keep her happy. You can always tell her, "You can't cut it!" after the show is over.

Do you do right by Tiffany and hire her at Fleece? Go to page 153.
Or do you do right by your wife, with whom you've rekindled some passion, and tell Tiffany to hit the bricks? Go to page 122.

You grab Diane's arm and stand up. The clerk looks up at you, clearly at a loss for what to do now. "She'll be right back," you say, and practically drag her toward the door and out on to the sidewalk. You square off with Diane, grab both of her arms, and barely restrain yourself from shaking her.

"Diane, what we're doing here . . ."

"What are we doing here?"

"You're right. I am never leaving my wife. It's true. You know me too well. But what we have is bigger and better than what I have with her. We're building a future here. I'm practically giving you two million dollars right now. I care more about you than I care about the PTA, Zabar's, and family reunions out in Quogue. This is my life, right here, right now. I'm sharing it with you and not with my wife. Don't screw this up for both of us. I love you, Diane."

Tears welling up in her eyes, she steps back, pushes slowly through the revolving doors, and walks back into the bank to sign the papers.

15 ↑1.75 ADLAC 22 ↓2.60 ENE 50.50 ↑1.50 TYC 60.25 ↓1.75 MSO 65 ↑2.

Go to page 134.

It's the next morning and you're sleeping late again. You had your second night in a row of sex with your wife—the first time that's happened since Apple was born.

You're watching CNBC to see what the final result of your bravado performance was. Claire Illustrado, the "Money Bunny," comes on the screen, and your ticker symbol—CON—pops up under her face. At that very moment your wife enters the bedroom with a cup of coffee.

"It was a Tuesday shocker for investors in Fleece Industries," says Illustrado, "as the company reported that it nearly met Wall Street's expectations, sending the stock skyrocketing."

"Look, honey, they might show me," you say to your wife. The two of you stare at the screen.

"But those same investors probably wish they had stayed in bed today."

Your wife looks at you with a curious expression. You shrug, but know deep down what Illustrado is about to say.

"Hank Snodgett, an analyst at Morgan Handey, did something last night that not too many analysts do anymore: He read Fleece's quarterly filing. And what he found has Wall Street screaming for blood. By using an arcane accounting rule, albeit a legal one, the company hid disappointing results from Asia and a growing number of returns by changing the way it accounts for its cost overruns. If they hadn't employed the tactic, their results would have come in forty-six-point-one percent below expectations, or almost three hundred million dollars less than their CEO claimed in an analyst meeting at the St. Regis. One attendee even told us that he smelled like liquor while he was giving his presentation."

5 ↑ 1.75 ADLAC 22 ↓ 2.60 ENE 50.50 ↑ 1.50 TYC 60.25 ↓ 1.75 MSO 65 ↑ 2.50

Go to page 160.

Murder? Who are you trying to kid? You're not that kind of person. And Weiss is an old friend. But you do need to think of something that will ensure his silence in the accounting matter.

Before you can dwell on your recent brush with murder, Araz Matali and Jeff McDougal, your marketing gurus, barge into your office. Deep down you know that McDougal and Matali are the key to Fleece's success. They have an uncanny ability to convince consumers of pretty much anything—straw hats in the wintertime or mink at a PETA conference. Whereas you used to spin fabric, after you brought these two on board, Fleece was spinning gold.

As they walk into your office they're already halfway into the conversation you were planning to have with them at the weekly marketing meeting, and you're forced to play catch-up. McDougal plops on the couch sipping a latte. Matali continues charging around the office, moving with such ferocity that tiny tornadoes emerge in his wake, lifting papers off your desk and causing the leaves of your ficus to flutter. He's clutching a *Details* magazine in his hand open to a page that pictures Adrien Brody leaning on the back bumper of a vintage Coup DeVille in what looks like a merino wool turtleneck.

"This two-bit actor has no loyalty to the people who make him look good! He knew he was supposed to wear a Fleece bowling shirt in this picture! The turtleneck contradicts the whole aesthetic of the retro look!"

"Blame the stylist, not the talent," McDougal chimes in.

"Please! Brody knew. I talked to him the day before this shoot about the shirt. I got him into P. Diddy's 'White Party' last summer, for God's sake! He owes me! Without me, he'd be doing donuts in the parking lot with Lizzie Grubman! He knew, Jeff!"

"Why don't you relax, Araz," says Jeff. "You hold on to things too tight. Our CEO is busy, and he doesn't want to hear about the ups and downs of being fashion's ambassador to the Hamptons."

McDougal is right. You couldn't care less, but you humor Araz because he's on your team, and if you're not his friend, how can he be yours?

"Araz, Jeff's right. I don't have time for this, but if it makes you feel better, I will sell my DVD of *The Pianist* on eBay."

"Burn it!" Araz screams, and then falls back against the wall, exhausted.

Go to page 5.

"Okay then, I suggest we get to work," says Moneyhouse as he puts his empty glass down on the table. *Damn*, you think, *the man can put them back.*

Moneyhouse stands up and snaps his fingers, and the waiter appears as if out of nowhere with a receipt for Moneyhouse to sign. It occurs to you that one of the fringe benefits of being in bed with this man might be your own tab at the Mercantile.

After signing the bill with a flourish, Moneyhouse strides for the door, saying, "We've got a conference room set up for a strategy meeting down at Moneyhouse and Stonecutter. We need to figure out a way to whitewash this accounting flim-flammery so that we can move forward in a more productive manner."

You and Barry follow him out into the piercing sunlight of a crisp fall day.

"I've got to get back to the office, boss," says Barry, hailing a cab and jumping in the door before you can protest.

"And you and I will take my limo back to my office," Moneyhouse says, opening the door and waiting impatiently for you to join him. As the limo pulls away from the curb, Moneyhouse slides open the liquor compartment, pulls out a bottle of Rémy, and pours two more drinks. *How does this man, who must be nearly drunk by now, make decisions that change the course of the economy?* you wonder. Not knowing how to refuse the drink, you take it from his outstretched hand. If you nurse it slowly, you might not have to drink much of it at all— Moneyhouse and Stonecutter is only a few blocks away.

Your cell phone rings. It's Fawn. "I've got Carson Rodriguez on the phone, and he says it's a huge emergency."

Carson Rodriguez? "I don't know anyone by that name," you say. "Who is he?"

Fawn laughs. "You don't know who Carson Rodriguez is? Don't you remember seeing him on the roof of the Soho House? He's that guy from *Fabulous Eye for the Corporate Guy.*

They're interior decorators for the executive elite. You've got to talk to him—here, I'll put him through."

Before you can hang up, you hear an overly enthusiastic voice come through the line. "How are you, you sassy success story? We've got to get going on your office. I'm looking at a picture of it now. What are you—a corporate titan or a frat guy who still thinks using milk crates as bookcases is cool? Come on now."

"Listen, I'm in the middle of something right now," you say. "Can we talk later?"

"There's no time," says Rodriguez. "I've already got a film crew lined up to visit the office tomorrow. So we need to make some decisions. Tuscan terra-cotta or old oaken London mustachio? What will it be?" You look at Moneyhouse, hoping to God that he can't hear the voice coming through your phone.

To your surprise, as Moneyhouse gulps down his second Rémy, he says, "I'd go with the terra-cotta. London mustachio is so yesterday."

"Is that Moneyhouse?" asks Rodriguez. "Tell him I still have a hangover."

You can't think of anything to do but say, "Sure, the terra-cotta," and you slam your phone shut.

15 ↑ 1.75 ADLAC 22 ↓ 2.60 ENE 50.50 ↑ 1.50 TYC 60.25 ↓ 1.75 MSO 65 ↑ 2.5

Go to page 208.

"Is everything okay?" you ask Flaxworthy. "You look upset."

"Oh, it's nothing," he says. "Office politics. There are ass-holes in every business. You know, I might be better put to use exposing the stupidity in the SEC itself." He laughs at his own joke, and you laugh with him. Maybe this is going to be easier than you thought.

"How about a cup of coffee?" you say, turning away from the conference room.

"Now, hold on. I'm a federal official," he says. "You do real-ize that bribery is a felony."

You freeze momentarily.

"Just kidding. I will have a coffee. Black."

You exhale, chuckling, and lean your head down the hallway. "Fawn, please get Mr. Flaxworthy a coffee. Black."

Minutes later, while Mr. Flaxworthy sips his coffee, you make small talk about Fleece's new licensing and cross-promotional activities.

"I do have other appointments today," Flaxworthy suddenly says, looking at his watch, "and since your counsel is not pres-ent, maybe we should meet again next week. Before I go, though, maybe we should step into your office to get your sig-nature on some forms."

"Let's do it," you say, wishing immediately that you could take those words back. That sniveling bastard Weiss is still in there, and who knows what kind of shape he's in. At this point, however, you're standing right outside your door, racking your brain to come up with an excuse. Without thinking, you begin the worst lie of your life.

"Fawn, are the painters still in my office?" Fawn looks up from her baked potato lunch with a mystified look. Before she can ask you what you're talking about, a commotion breaks out by the elevators. You hear what must be the doors of the display cabinet being ripped from their hinges.

"Where is he? I've got a message for him!" There's a crash.

Flaxworthy is clearly panicked, and you are momentarily thankful for the diversion.

Barry rumbles around the corner and bangs into Fawn's desk, planting his right palm in her out-box. He's clearly drunk and most definitely angry.

Go to page 187.

After another half hour of convincing your wife that you are not the liar that you actually are, you head to the office. You know exactly what you have to do.

"Fawn, get Baldacker in here immediately."

A few minutes later Baldacker walks into your office.

"Leave the door open!" you say. "This won't take long."

He looks at you and says, "Shouldn't we be trying to figure out how to handle this?"

"Handle what?" you respond. "How could you do this to us? To Fleece? To me? We're the laughingstock of Wall Street, all because of some accounting scam you tried to run. What the hell were you thinking? Didn't we talk about team-work?"

Baldacker looks confused for a few more seconds. And then all of a sudden his face turns into one big scowl.

"If you think I'm taking the fall for this, you're insane," he sneers at you. "You approved that decision. Two days ago. In this very office. If you think I'm going down alone, you're out of your mind."

"Fawn, Baldacker is getting out of control in here," you say, as you turn your back to him. "Call Nevins and get security up here immediately. He's terminated."

The next few months are full of turmoil. The Securities and Exchange Commission contacted you shortly after Snodgett's report. They tell you that you aren't a "suspect," but merely a "person of interest." Encouraged by your lawyer, Johnny Conran, you take the classic head-in-the-sand defense. You manage to convince investigators of the "plausible deniability" doctrine that would be tough for them to disprove.

Your reputation takes a beating, but like many a tarnished CEO, you come to realize that America was founded on second chances. The mea culpa sale that you run right after the SEC drops its investigation is a blowout hit, and your remark to a reporter, "I barely escaped the gallows pole," even makes you a quirky cult hero among the chattering classes. In the end, you reaffirm the golden rule of modern America: There are different rules for CEOs—much, much more lenient rules.

The end

One Wednesday morning you're at work looking over some new designs for the Department of Homeland Security. Araz and Jeff are buzzing about your office as usual.

"Terrorists, meet the fashion police!" says Araz.

"Isn't 'fashion police' a derogatory term?" asks Jeff.

"Not anymore! It's a patriotic American term from now on," says Araz, who isn't even American.

This contract will be worth a fortune to Fleece, and you've already spent the bonus you'll give yourself for it on a Peter Max painting. Carson went to Baton Rouge to close the deal for you on Monday, and you're waiting to hear from him about when you can send someone up to New Hampshire to pick it up.

The phone rings. Fawn comes over the intercom. "Carson Rodriguez for you."

"Ask him if the painting has arrived in New Hampshire," you say in response. "I can't talk to him now, but tell him thanks for me."

"He says he really needs to talk to you."

You grab the phone. "Carson, I'm busy right now, can you call me back?"

"I can't," he says. "They say I'm only allowed to make one phone call."

Carson is in jail? For what? And why is he calling you?

Go to page 52.

Once outside the building, you start walking away from the water-front. You don't realize it at first, but you're unconsciously walking toward 120 Broadway, the office of the New York State attorney general, Craven Albanie. You arrive just five minutes later and ask the heavyset receptionist if you can speak to Mr. Albanie.

"He's not taking any visitors right now," she says, in between bites of an Atkins wrap and swigs of a Diet Coke. "Can I tell him who's here?"

"Tell him it's the CEO of Fleece Industries," you respond. She picks up her phone, says something you can't hear, and then looks up. "He'll see you now. Just down the hallway on your left."

You realize that this short walk will effectively be your last steps as the CEO of a public company. It feels like walking to the principal's office. The hallway has the same officious cold-ness of a high school, and it occurs to you that government buildings are eerily similar to educational and correctional facil-ities—bleak, cold, and blue-green.

You knock and open the door. Craven Albanie gets up from his desk. "This is a surprise. I don't know whether congratulations are due—your IPO was spectacular—or whether you're here for different reasons. Tell me I can congratulate you," he says.

"I'm afraid not, Mr. Albanie. It will be me congratulating you instead. This is the case you've been waiting for, the one that will put you in the governor's mansion. As for me, I've always tried to do the right thing, in business and in life. So, here it is: Fleece Industries is a complete sham."

You explain the whole situation—Weiss, Moneyhouse, even the terra-cotta office idea—all to Albanie's joyful ears. It feels good to get it off your chest, and it feels even better when Albanie tells you what a good person you are and how he'll do everything in his power to represent you as a Wall Street golden boy to the press. Your future, though less lucrative, will definitely not be as terrible as you had feared.

Go to page 247.

"Your Honor, we regret to inform the court that we have come to an impasse. The jury is deadlocked and we cannot come to a consensus. One juror could not be swayed." The foreman's gaze oscillates between the judge and the Librarian as he gives the verdict of a hung jury.

"Mr. Foreman, I will ask you to speak no more. And I declare this case a mistrial. Sir, it pains me to say this to you after I have listened to all of the evidence, and I know that you are not as impervious to fault as your Silk Armor clothing line. Nevertheless, I have no recourse but to let you off. I hope I never see you in my courtroom again."

The next morning you wake up in room 318 with Diane sleeping at your side. You rise, naked, and walk to your hotel room door. You open the door and look down at your waiting *New York Post.*

SILK ARMOR DEFENSE IMPENETRABLE

You pick up the paper and notice a maid pushing a cleaning cart down the hall. She notices your naked body and puts her hand over her mouth. You wave at her politely and shut the door.

The end

You immediately head toward Weiss's office. As you approach his door you notice that the lights aren't on, though Weiss is sitting at his desk in the dark, staring at the flying toasters on his screen saver. He's startled by your appearance in his doorway, and when you flip the light switch on, you notice that he's been crying.

"Weiss, what's wrong with you? Didn't I tell you everything was going to be okay? That you have been—and will remain—an integral part of the team?"

He rubs the back of his wrist across his nose. "Yeah, I guess so, boss, but you hired that woman this morning, and I'm not so dumb that I can't read the writing on the wall."

"Wrong wall, Weiss, wrong wall. Listen, you fucked up—big time. But you're family, and families stick together. If there's one thing Fleece has over every other publicly traded company, it's loyalty. I'll cover your ass, but you've got to cover mine. I'm going to need you to go to Australia for our spring launch at the Open. Briana Ponastova will most certainly need an escort, both during the day and at all of our parties, and you're actually the perfect guy for the job. Aren't you a Ponastova fan?"

You've never actually seen a man shift from crying to drooling in such short order—Weiss is ecstatic. A few more words of encouragement and you're comfortable with the fact that he's back on board and won't be telling anybody anything.

When you open the door to leave his office, you walk into a cloud of cigarette smoke that seems to be hovering right outside the door. But nobody's there.

↑ 1.75 ADLAC 22 ↓ 2.60 ENE 50.50 ↑ 1.50 TYC 60.25 ↓ 1.75 MSO 65 ↑ 2.50

Go to page 109.

Six months later you're on Page Six, along with Starr, Antoinette, the street magician, and a host of jam bands. And the news is not good: Ciccone has been busted for running a Ponzi scheme, effectively borrowing from Peter to pay Paul. His investment company was a sham set up to fund his own extravagant lifestyle, and if investors ever asked for their money back, he just recruited a new client and paid the outgoing client with the new monies. All of your money is gone; Ciccone had used it to pay out some white rapper from Seattle.

Ciccone even tried to jump bail but was arrested at JFK airport with a suitcase full of small bills and a one-way ticket to Rome. The man hasn't lost his gall, either. After the story broke, Giancarlo DaVinci, one of his clients, bad-mouthed Ciccone in an interview with the *New York Times*. He responded by suing DaVinci for slander.

In one year your whole life has spun out in a 180-degree turn. Once a hero, you're now a goat. The press takes you to task for being another in the never-ending list of CEOs who accept huge cash payouts while the little guy continues to get screwed. You're ultimately ousted from Fleece by the very board that granted you the bonus, with Ken Hart explaining to reporters that they were working off of "incomplete information" when they'd given you the $10 million.

Even Apple suffers. The Marriott girls refuse to hang out with her anymore because of the "stench of scandal" surrounding the family name. As a result, she doesn't get to be in an episode of their reality TV series, *The Suite Life*, and doesn't speak to you for six months.

Your wife divorces you, marries Ken Hart, and moves to Tuscany.

The end

The hallway is dark and smells like a combination of beer and fear. The fat biker leads you down a set of stairs into the basement, where Lynyrd Skynyrd is blaring, and the meanest-looking group of people you have ever seen in your life are standing around a pool table. Just then Rampstein stands up and starts walking toward you.

"Thanks for coming," he starts. "I'm really sorry to have asked you to come down here on such short notice, but after more than thirty years of bumming around the country, trying to find my sanity again, I suddenly found I was short on cash. Then I saw you on TV today. Did you have any idea these guys would be the type to watch CNNfn?"

You don't know whether to answer the question, so you just stare back at him.

"Cat got your tongue? That's okay. I saw a lot of my friends have theirs cut out by the Vietcong while I was a POW. I can do all the talking. Let's see. I think a million dollars will do for now. We can talk about the long-term payment plan later on. But I want to see you transfer the money into my bank account over the Internet right now."

He points into the corner, where there's a surprisingly well-appointed setup of computer, flat-screen monitor, and speaker system.

"We even have Wi-Fi," says one of the bikers, seemingly reading your mind.

You snap out of your shock. "Rampstein, wake up. I can't transfer a million dollars on the Internet. I don't even have a million dollars. All my money is in Fleece stock."

"Which leg do you want us to break first?" he asks, calmly removing his jacket. You look around and notice that you are in the center of a circle of very menacing men. You decide you have to get out of there. You grab the pool cue out of the fat biker's chubby pink fist and swing it wildly, hitting Aaron in the head.

"Ouch, that hurt," he says, still in the same calm voice. "But I probably would have tried the same thing."

You swing at him again, but he catches the cue and pulls it out of your hand. Out of nowhere, he's holding a blackjack above your face. He brings it smashing down onto your nose, which explodes in a torrent of blood. When you regain your senses, he's standing above you, holding a pair of nunchucks.

Before you can tell him that you'll pay whatever he wants, one stick comes crashing down onto your jaw, which makes a strange popping sound as it separates itself from the rest of your face. Then the other crushes your cheek. He wraps the nunchucks around your neck and starts to strangle you. Your last thought before you die is: *I hope they find me with clothes on.*

The end

Two months down the road, you are in your limo on the way to your new office as New York's lieutenant governor. You read the following headline on the front page of the *New York Times:*

**WALL STREET'S GOLDEN BOY WALKS AWAY FROM
FORTUNE TO DEDICATE SELF TO PUBLIC SERVICE!**

The end